AN **OFFICIAL BOOK** INSPIRED BY THE FILMS

Harry Potter™

BAKE, CREATE, AND DECORATE!

WIZARDING
WORLD®

AN **OFFICIAL BOOK** INSPIRED BY THE FILMS

Harry Potter ™

BAKE, CREATE, AND DECORATE!

⁕ ⋯ BY ⋯ ⁕

Joanna Farrow

SCHOLASTIC INC.

WIZARDING WORLD®

CONTENTS

CUPCAKES AND CAKE POPS

WIZARDING SKILL LEVEL

To help guide you, we've given each of our recipes a lightning bolt difficulty rating, from one (beginner) all the way to three (advanced).

⚡ BEGINNER

⚡⚡ INTERMEDIATE

⚡⚡⚡ ADVANCED

CONTENTS

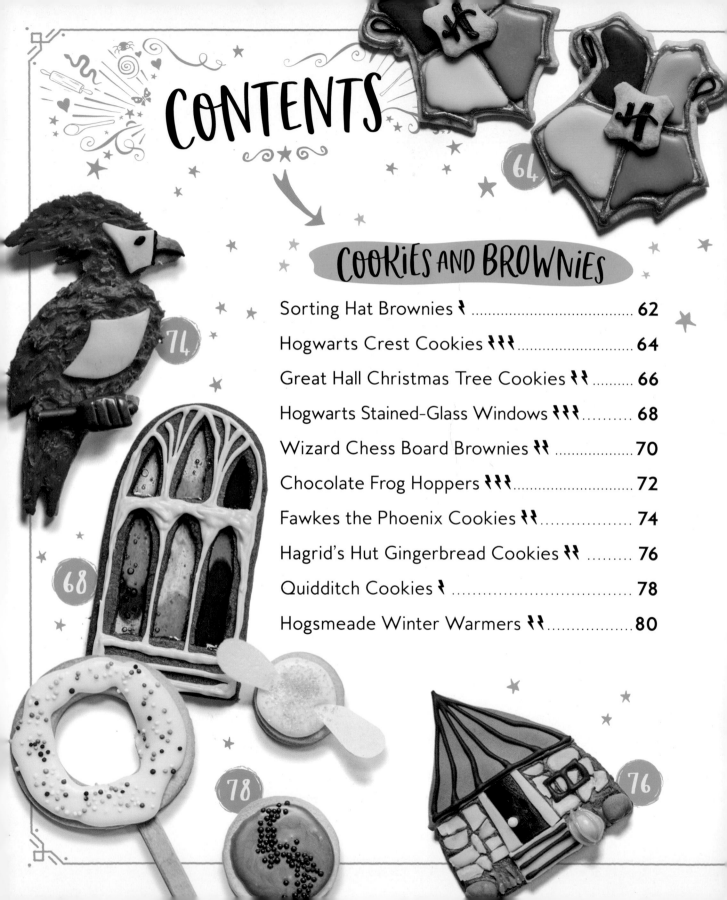

COOKIES AND BROWNIES

BASIC RECIPES

BASIC RECIPES ICON

Look out for this icon throughout the book. Whenever you see it, it means you have the choice of creating an ingredient (like frosting or cake) yourself using the basic recipes at the back of the book, purchasing it ready-made, or making it from a pre-made mix.

LET'S BAKE, CREATE, AND DECORATE!

The wizarding world is full of scrumptious treats. From foaming tankards of Butterbeer to the buzz of Fizzing Whizzbees, the food seen in the Harry Potter films is every bit as enchanting as the spells. These tasty treats always look fantastic too. The aim of this book is to help you create your own magic whenever you step into the kitchen, baking and decorating masterpieces delicious enough to make any witch's or wizard's mouth water!

Bake, Create, and Decorate is a little bit different from other creative baking books. That's because you can either make all the creations yourself, with the help of our Basic Recipes at the back of the book, use a pre-made mix, or buy a cake, cupcakes, cookies, or icings that are already made. When it comes to the decorating, you will find step-by-step instructions on every recipe to guide you. You can also add personal flair by playing with color, flavor, and shape. For example, you can design your own Ollivanders wand (pages 24–25), draw your own Marauder's Map (pages 30–31), or even create different dragon breeds (pages 54–55). The only limit is your imagination!

Aside from the fact that they're all delicious, another great thing about the recipes included in this book is that they're great for sharing. Why not whip up some of these bakes to enjoy at a movie night, to serve as a tasty after-dinner dessert, or to add a touch of magic to a party?

Before starting your bakes, read through the instructions carefully, checking you have all the necessary ingredients and utensils. Always ask an adult for help when using sharp tools or hot equipment. You will spot symbols beside each recipe where you might need some extra assistance.

Are you ready to embark on a delicious adventure? Then, gather your ingredients, grab your apron, raise your wands (or wooden spoons!), and get decorating.

Let the magic begin!

BAKING BASICS

The recipes in this book are designed to be easy to follow. But here are some extra tips to make things even simpler.

BAKING TIPS

◆ It can be tricky knowing when to take your bake out of the oven. It's not always possible to judge by appearance. If your cake or brownie looks (and smells!) done, gently poke a toothpick or fork into the center. If it comes out clean, you're ready!

◆ Once you've made cookie dough, pop it in the fridge to firm up. This will make it much easier to roll out and shape your delicious cookies.

PARCHMENT PAPER

The students at Hogwarts use parchment to write notes during lessons. But in the kitchen, you can use parchment paper (sometimes known as baking parchment) to stop your cakes and cookies from sticking. Cut the paper to size so it lines the bottom of your cake pans and baking sheets. It can help to grease cake pans before adding batter too. Just don't forget to remove the parchment paper from your bakes before you begin to decorate!

Wingardium Leviosa

DECORATING TiPS

⬥ Always allow your bakes to cool completely before decorating. Adding frosting or fondant too soon could cause it to melt and skew your designs. Cakes can cool in their pans.

⬥ Piping can be intimidating, but there's no need to be worried. Practice piping onto parchment paper before starting your creation. This can help you figure out the correct spacing and sizing of your writing or decorations. Gently apply even pressure to the piping bag, taking your time. And if you make a mistake, you can always scrape the icing off and try again!

FOOD COLORiNG

To capture the vivid colors of the Wizarding World, some of these recipes use natural food coloring. You can find food coloring in most grocery stores. You can get creative and mix colors to create even more color options too! But take care—working with food coloring can get messy! Start small, applying only a couple of drops and gradually building to get the desired color. Wash your hands thoroughly after use and always wear an apron to prevent staining.

TEMPLATES

Templates for some of the recipes are included in the back of this book. To create a stencil, carefully trace the image onto a piece of plain paper or parchment paper, then carefully cut out the shape with scissors. Simply place the template over your dough or fondant then gently cut around it to create your final shape.

ESSENTIAL EQUIPMENT

Every young witch and wizard makes a trip to Diagon Alley to get their school supplies. But for this book, you can find most of what you need in a grocery store! Here are a few tools that would be useful to get your hands on:

Piping bags and tips

Scales

Rolling pin

Oven mitts

Measuring cups

Cupcake/muffin pan

Cutting board

Spatula

Measuring spoons

Cupcake liners in various colors

Loaf pan

Parchment paper

Baking sheet

Cooling rack

Scissors

Ruler

Cake pan

Large plates or boards to build and present your creations on

Wooden spoon

Range of mixing bowls

Electric mixer

FROSTING AND ICING

Let's take a quick look at the different types
of frosting used in this book:

BUTTERCREAM

Buttercream is a thick, sweet frosting made from butter and sugar. It is great for coating the outside of a cake or filling the inside. It can be spread out with a spatula or palette knife for a smooth look, or lifted into peaks to create texture. It can also be piped from a bag.

ROYAL ICING

Royal icing is smoother than buttercream frosting and has a lovely glossy finish. Made from egg whites and sugar, it is perfect for skilled decorations, such as "flooding," where cookies are covered in a smooth layer of icing for a professional look.

FONDANT

A thick icing typically used to cover cakes, fondant is both tasty and useful, particularly when sculpting figures or decorations. It can be rolled and remodeled into almost any shape. When working with fondant, be sure to keep your hands clean and dry. Water makes fondant very sticky!

GLACÉ ICING

A simple recipe of sugar and water, glacé icing is smooth and runny. It can be made thicker by adjusting the ingredient levels, making it adaptable to suit your bake!

KITCHEN SAFETY

It's important to be properly prepared before making magic in the kitchen. Here are some handy tips to follow to stay safe while baking.

Tip #1

Read the recipe carefully from start to finish. It is helpful to know the cooking order before starting your bake.

Tip #2

Look at all the necessary ingredients and utensils before you begin to make sure you have everything you need. Keep them in easy reach!

Tip #3

Clean the area where you'll be working before you begin—and be sure to tidy up afterward to prevent the spread of germs.

Tip #4

Wash your hands thoroughly with soap and water, then dry them with a clean towel.

Tip #5

Put on an apron to protect your clothing. Tie up long hair or pin it back.

Tip #6

When using a knife, make sure it fits your hand comfortably and hold the knife firmly by the handle. Make sure the sharp side of the blade is pointing down and always chop away from you.

Tip #7

Always wear protective mitts when using the oven. Ask an adult for help whenever you see one of the below symbols on a step!

Tip #8

Be sure food is baked thoroughly, and never serve piping hot treats. Let your creations cool before digging in.

OLDER MUGGLES ONLY ALERT

If you see either or both of these symbols on a recipe, it means an adult should be present to help keep everyone safe.

 Using knives and sharp tools

 Using the oven and handling hot utensils

LARGE CAKES

Bertie Bott's Every Flavour Beans Box
Deathly Hallows Cake
Knight Bus Layer Cake
Ollivanders Wands
Cauldron Cake
Welcome Feast Illusion Cake
Marauder's Map Cake
Hogwarts House Scarf Cake
Harry's Birthday Cake
Hogwarts: A History Cake

BERTIE BOTT'S EVERY FLAVOUR BEANS BOX

Harry's first experience eating Bertie Bott's Every Flavour Beans was on the Hogwarts Express in the first film. He came across some very interesting flavors! If you can't get a hold of these quirky sweets, use regular jelly beans instead.

ABOUT 1 HOUR | **SERVES 10-12**

- Vanilla Sponge Cake (approximately 11 x 7 inch/28 x 18 cm)
- 12 oz/350 g Buttercream Frosting
- Several rolls of red fruit leather, ribbons, or sour strips
- Handful of soft yellow fruit jelly candies/sweets
- 1 soft green fruit jelly candy
- 1 soft orange fruit jelly candy
- Yellow sugar sprinkles
- Tube of black decorator frosting/icing
- 3 small yellow sugar stars
- Approximately ½ cup/100 g jelly beans

SPECIAL EQUIPMENT
Small spatula/palette knife

Ruler, optional

1

Turn the cooled, **baked cake** (see page 86) onto a flat board or plate. Cut two corners off the top of the cake to create the pointed top of the box. Take a very thin slice off the remaining three sides of the cake to neaten the edges.

2

Spread the **buttercream** (see page 88) over the top and sides of the cake until it's covered in an even layer. Use a spatula to smooth the frosting as neatly as possible. Then use the tip of the spatula to draw a window in the center of the cake, about 3½ inches/9 cm on each side.

TOP TIP

You'll need to roll the fruit jelly candies quite firmly to flatten them. If they curl up, leave for a few minutes and then try again!

3 Lay ¼ inch/5 mm strips of **red fruit leather** over the frosted cake as shown in the photograph. (If the fruit leather is too wide, cut it into thinner strips using scissors.) Trim the ends with scissors as needed to fit on the cake. Leave the area clear within the window and make sure you have two long red strips on either side of the window as these will support the yellow pillars.

4 Using a rolling pin, thinly roll out some **yellow fruit jellies**. Cut out two triangular shapes and four rectangular shapes for the tops and bases of the pillars using a small sharp knife or scissors. Roll out and shape three long rectangles for under the window.

MAGICAL FACT

A favorite with Hogwarts students, these colorful sweets really do come in every flavor, including chocolate, peppermint, spinach, liver, and tripe. According to Ron, George Weasley once got a bogey-flavored one. YUCK!

5 Thinly roll out a **green, orange**, and **yellow fruit jelly** and then cut out elongated triangles for the party hat. Position the candies on the cake as shown.

Use your fingers to sprinkle the **yellow sugar sprinkles** into the space between the fruit leather to complete the pillars. Add as many sprinkles as you can without them spilling over the edges of the fruit leather.

Use the **black decorator frosting** to pipe outlines around the pillars. Then outline the window, add lines to the hat, and write "Every Flavour Beans" on the yellow rectangles under the window. Position a **yellow sugar star** at the top of each pillar and the party hat. Scatter the **jelly beans** within the window, piling them up a little in the center.

19

DEATHLY HALLOWS CAKE

Just like the Deathly Hallows—the Elder Wand, the Resurrection Stone, and the Cloak of Invisibility—the ingredients in this recipe work together in tandem, and the end result is something very delicious indeed. If you'd prefer to use other candies for your cake's center, just make sure they're small enough to sprinkle.

45-60 MINS | **SERVES 12**

 Chocolate Sponge Cake (approximately 11 x 7 inches/ 28 x 18 cm)

 12 oz/350 g Chocolate Buttercream Frosting

¾-1 cup/125-150 g chocolate-covered raisins, candy-coated chocolates, or other small chocolate candies/sweets

Approximately ⅓ cup/80 g chocolate or gold sprinkles

SPECIAL EQUIPMENT

Small spatula/palette knife

5½ inch/14 cm round cutter, cake tin, or bowl

Once your **cake** (see page 86) is baked and cooled, trim the edges of the cake to neaten them, then cut the cake diagonally in half. Flip one half over and position the pieces close together so they make a triangle shape.

Use the yellow dotted lines as a cutting guide.

1.

2. Flip one half over.

3. Position the two halves together to make a triangle.

2

Use a spatula to spread a little **buttercream** (see page 88) into the gap between the cakes and gently push the two halves together. Spread the remaining buttercream all over the top and sides of the cake until it's covered in an even layer. Spread as smoothly as possible using the spatula.

3

Gently place a 5½ inch/14 cm round cutter, cake tin, or bowl over the center of the cake. Carefully lift it away to leave a neat circle in the middle of the triangle. Use the tip of the spatula to mark a line from the top of the cake down through the center of the circle to complete the Deathly Hallows symbol.

4

Use the **chocolate-covered raisins** to decorate the edges of the cake, along the center line, and around the marked circle by pressing them very lightly into the buttercream.

TOP TIP

If you don't have chocolate or gold sprinkles, you can swap them for finely grated milk or dark chocolate. Alternatively, mini colored candies, not much larger than sugar sprinkles, would add a bit of color to this impressive cake.

5

Sprinkle the **chocolate or gold sprinkles** into the center of the circle, spreading them in an even layer.

KNIGHT BUS LAYER CAKE

As Stan Shunpike said: "Welcome to the Knight Bus!" You'll feel just like Harry Potter in the third film when you cut into this lookalike cake with delicious, stripy layers, sandwiched with buttercream frosting. This magical triple-decker bus would make a fabulous centerpiece for any important Muggle occasion.

1½–2 HOURS | **SERVES 20**

 2 Vanilla Sponge Cakes (approximately 11 x 7 inch/ 28 x 18 cm each)

 12 oz/350 g Buttercream Frosting

Purple natural food coloring

Pack of wafer cookies/wafers

4 mini chocolate sandwich cookies/ biscuits

Small piece licorice

Tubes of yellow and white decorator frosting/icing

2 small round yellow gumdrops/gums

SPECIAL EQUIPMENT

Small spatula/palette knife

 Start with your two baked, cooled **cakes** (see pages 86–87). If the cakes are slightly domed in the center, carefully cut a thin horizontal slice off each using a large knife. Cut each cake into three even-sized rectangles.

TOP TIP

If you are making your own vanilla cakes for this recipe, you can add a few drops of purple food coloring to one of the batters before baking. You won't be able to have purple layers if using bought, ready-made cakes, but it'll still taste delicious.

Place a **purple rectangle** on the center of a flat plate or board and thinly spread with a little **buttercream** (see page 88). Position an uncolored cake rectangle on top and spread this with a little buttercream. Place another purple cake layer in position, making sure all the cakes sit squarely over the cake below.

Continue layering the **cakes**, spreading each with a thin layer of **buttercream** and finishing with an uncolored cake layer. Use a knife to trim the cake at both ends and on the sides if necessary so the edges are neat. This will make it easier to decorate.

Add a few drops of **purple food coloring** into the remaining buttercream and stir until evenly colored. Spread the frosting over the sides and the top of the cake in an even layer. Use one hand to gently support the top of the cake so it doesn't wobble! Spread the buttercream as smoothly as you can with a small spatula.

MAGICAL FACT

If you've seen *Harry Potter and the Prisoner of Azkaban*, you'll know that the Knight Bus travels at breakneck speeds—much to Harry's astonishment. To achieve this effect, the vehicles around the bus drove very slowly during filming while the bus was driven as fast as was safe. The footage was then sped up further in post-production.

Press the **wafer cookies** into the sides, front, and back of the cake for the windows. If the wafer cookies are thick, you might need to cut them with a small, sharp knife. You might also need to cut them into sections to fit the length of the cake. Position the **chocolate sandwich cookies** at the cake corners for wheels.

Using a small knife, cut the **licorice** into a small rectangle and press it to the front of the cake at the base for the radiator grille. Cut another rectangle and write "Knight Bus" on it with **white decorator frosting**. Push a **yellow gumdrop** into place on each side of the grille. Use the **yellow decorator frosting** to pipe outlines around the windows and grille.

OLLIVANDERS WANDS

Take inspiration from Ollivanders wand shop with these magically scrumptious brownie bars. The photograph shows the wands belonging to Hermione, Snape, and Harry, though you can get creative and copy the wands of any of your favorite characters or even create your own. Just remember: the wand chooses the wizard, not the other way around!

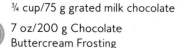
🕐 1½ HOURS   🍴 SERVES 12

 Chocolate Brownie (approximately 9 inches/23 cm square)

¾ cup/75 g grated milk chocolate

 7 oz/200 g Chocolate Buttercream Frosting

Plenty of thin tubular fruit leather or strips

5 oz/150 g purple fondant

Confectioners'/icing sugar for dusting

3 thin breadsticks, around 8-9 inches/20-23 cm long

2 oz/50 g ivory/white fondant

 1

Cut the **brownies** (see page 85) into three even-sized slabs so you have one for each wand. Scatter the **grated milk chocolate** onto a piece of paper or small tray.

MAGICAL FACT

Over the course of 10 years of filming, it is thought that Daniel Radcliffe (who played Harry) broke around 70 wands. That certainly would have kept Garrick Ollivander (played in the films by the late John Hurt) busy.

2

Using a small round bladed knife, spread the sides of each **brownie** slab with **chocolate buttercream** (see page 88), reserving a little for the tops. Carefully take one slab and use your fingers to press the **grated milk chocolate** gently over the sides until thinly coated. Transfer to a large flat plate or board while you coat the remaining two slabs in the same way.

3

Spread the tops with the remaining **buttercream**. Use the **fruit leather** or strips to decorate the top edges of each of the slabs. Cut down to fit where necessary with scissors or a small knife.

4

Divide the **purple fondant** into three pieces. Roll out one at a time on a surface lightly dusted with **confectioners' sugar** and cut out a rectangle measuring about 7 x 3 inches/18 x 7.5 cm.

5

Score the rectangle about ¼ inch/5 mm from the edges with the tip of a knife to decorate and drape over one of the slabs, lifting the edges in places to resemble fabric. Decorate the remainder in the same way.

6

Decorate the **breadsticks** with **ivory fondant** as in the photographs. For Hermione's wand, roll out a long strip of fondant under the palms of your hands, making it thicker toward one end. Wrap around a breadstick so the thicker end of the fondant is at the base of the breadstick. Position on one of the boxes.

7

For Snape's wand, wrap a small piece of **fondant** around the end of a **breadstick**. Roll the fondant over a textured surface such as a metal grater. Wrap thin bands of fondant at the ends and score the center of the wand handle with the tip of a knife. Shape Harry's wand in the same way, scoring texture into the handle with the tip of a knife.

CAULDRON CAKE

It takes a very special type of student to whip up a batch of Polyjuice Potion in only their second year at Hogwarts, but then Hermione Granger is no ordinary witch. Now you can have a go at your own "potion making" with this creamy Cauldron Cake. And the best bit is that it tastes as delicious as it looks!

🕐 **1½ HOURS**   🍴🍽️ **SERVES 10**

 3 Vanilla Sponge Cakes (approximately 6 inches/15 cm in diameter)

4 tbsp strawberry or raspberry jam

 12 oz/350 g Buttercream Frosting

16-20 chocolate finger cookies/ biscuits

Black, orange, and yellow natural food colorings

3½ oz/100 g dark gray fondant

Confectioners'/icing sugar, for dusting

Green sugar sprinkles

1 tbsp granulated sugar

SPECIAL EQUIPMENT

½ inch/1 cm star piping tube

Large paper or plastic piping bag

Small spatula/palette knife

1. Stack your cooled, **baked cakes** (see pages 86–87) on top of one another. Using a knife, carefully cut away the sides of the cake in a curve, so you end up with a shape that looks like a ball with a flat top. Carefully cut away a little at a time until you're happy with the shape.

2. Gently separate the layers and spread the bottom layer with half the **jam** in a thin layer and a heaping spoonful of the **buttercream** (see page 88) spread over the top. Position the middle layer on top and spread with the remaining jam and another spoonful of buttercream. Position the final cake on top.

Layer orange and yellow buttercream in your piping bag to get a piped flame effect!

Arrange the **chocolate finger cookies** on the center of a flat board or plate, cutting some in half to resemble logs. Lower the cake on top.

Add a few drops of **black food coloring** to half the remaining **buttercream** and mix until it turns dark gray. Divide the rest of the buttercream in half again, and color half orange using **orange food coloring**. Color the last of the buttercream yellow using **yellow food coloring**. Place alternate spoonfuls of the orange and yellow frosting in a large piping bag fitted with a ½ inch/1 cm star tube. Set aside.

Using a small spatula, spread the **gray buttercream** all over the sides of the cake, using one hand to gently support the top. Spread the frosting as smoothly as possible with the spatula, finishing with a little more frosting on the top. Don't worry if the base of the cake is a little untidy— it will be covered with more frosting!

Take the piping bag of **frosting** and pipe flames around the base of the cake between the chocolate cookies. Pull the bag away slightly as you pipe to make the flame shapes longer. Roll out the **gray fondant** on a surface dusted with **confectioners' sugar** and cut out a strip measuring 11 x ½ inch/28 x 1 cm. Lift the strip and arrange it around the top of the cake in a circle to create the cauldron rim. Press the ends lightly together.

Gather up the trimmings and roll them on the surface under the palms of your hands into a long thin rope. Cut off the ends so the rope is 10 inches/25.5 cm long and drape it around the cake, securing the ends over the rim to create a handle.

Fill the top of the cauldron with **green sugar sprinkles** and a swirl of **granulated sugar**.

TOP TIP
Take your time with step 1 by cutting away just a little of the cake at a time. You can always take more away, but you can't put it back!

WELCOME FEAST ILLUSION CAKE

Is it really a plateful of turkey drumstick, fries, carrots, and peas, complete with a hearty dollop of gravy? No. Much like a clever bit of Transfiguration, this tasty treat is really a sponge cake in disguise. What else would you expect in such a magical place as Hogwarts's Great Hall, where the ceiling itself seems to be alive?

🕐 1½–2 HOURS   🍽 SERVES 20

- 2 Vanilla Sponge Cakes (approximately 7 x 3½ inches/ 18 x 9 cm each)
- Confectioners'/icing sugar, for dusting
- 1½ oz/40 g white fondant
- 1 plain or chocolate-covered pretzel stick, about 5 inches/ 13 cm long
- ½ cup/50 g crushed cookie/biscuit crumbs

- 7 oz/200 g Buttercream Frosting
- Handful of soft green and orange fruit chews
- 4-5 tbsp caramel or fudge pouring sauce

1 Place one of your baked, cooled **cakes** (see pages 86-87) on a cutting board or work surface. Using a small, sharp knife, cut away the edges and corners of the sponge until you have a shape that resembles a turkey drumstick. Make the shape thinner at one end for attaching the turkey bone. Make sure you trim a small amount of cake at a time until you are happy with the shape.

2 Cut slices from the **second cake**. Work slowly and carefully so you don't make too many crumbs. Then cut the slices across into chunky "fries." Arrange the fries in a pile toward the back of a large flat plate or board.

3

Dust your fingers lightly with **confectioners' sugar** and mold the **fondant** into a bone end shape as in the photograph. Once you're happy with the shape, push one end of the **pretzel** into the fondant from the thin end until it almost comes out the other side. Place to one side on a piece of parchment paper while you prepare the drumstick.

4

Tip the **cookie crumbs** out onto a surface in a thin layer. Spread the top of the shaped **sponge** with **buttercream** (see page 88) using a round-bladed knife. Turn it onto the plate of crumbs and spread the rest of the cake with buttercream so it's completely covered. Carefully turn the cake in the crumbs until fully coated.

(see page 88)

MAGICAL FACT

Students are treated to a magnificent Welcome Feast every September 1. The tables magically fill with plates of food after Professor Dumbledore greets the students for the new school year.

5

Position the **cake** so the thin end rests on top of the pile of fries. Take the **shaped fondant** bone and push the **pretzel** into the narrow end of the cake to secure it in place.

6

Unwrap all the **fruit chews**. Cut each green chew into 5-6 pieces and shape into peas. Halve each orange chew diagonally and shape them into carrots. Place in a pile beside the cake. Pour the **caramel** or **fudge sauce** into a bowl and check the consistency: It should thinly coat the back of a spoon—like gravy! If necessary, thin with a few drops of cold water. Just before serving, drizzle the sauce over the cake.

MARAUDER'S MAP CAKE

Is that Harry wandering the Hogwarts corridors, Dumbledore pacing in his office, or someone more sinister? This cake is a simplified version of the Marauder's Map Harry receives from Fred and George Weasley in the third film. You only have a little fine detail to do, but it still requires a steady hand. And, of course, you'll need to solemnly swear that you are up to no good before beginning!

1 HOUR **SERVES 12**

 Vanilla Sponge Cake (approximately 11 x 7 inches/ 28 x 18 cm)

 12 oz/350 g Chocolate Buttercream Frosting

Confectioners'/icing sugar, for dusting

9 oz/250 g white fondant

2 tbsp chocolate sprinkles

½ tsp instant coffee granules

Black natural food coloring

SPECIAL EQUIPMENT

Small spatula/palette knife

Fine paintbrush

Pastry brush

1

Turn the cooled, baked **cake** (see page 86) onto a large flat plate or board and trim the edges to neaten if necessary. Spread the **buttercream** (see page 88) over the top and sides of the cake. Spread as neatly as possible with a spatula.

2

On a surface generously dusted with **confectioners' sugar**, roll out the **fondant** into a rectangle that's the same size as the measurements of the cake. Trim off the edges to neaten. To draw the map, take a pinch of **chocolate sprinkles** and place them down on the fondant (see Top Tip).

Continue to take pinches of the **chocolate sprinkles** and arrange them on the **fondant** to create straight lines, curved ones, and any other shapes you like. Build up the map with more sprinkles until you're happy with the design. Brush the sprinkles aside or clean up the shapes with a pastry brush.

Gently press a rolling pin over the **fondant** to press the **sprinkles** into it.

Carefully lift the **white fondant** onto the **cake** and position it as centrally as you can. You can crumple up the edges of the white fondant by sliding a round-bladed knife underneath the fondant, lifting and pulling it out toward the edges of the cake carefully so that you don't get **buttercream** all over the white fondant.

Dissolve the **coffee granules** in a small bowl with 1 tablespoon boiling water. Dip the pastry brush into the coffee, remove as much as you can on the edge of the bowl, and lightly paint the **fondant** in patches to create an aged look to the map. If you're unsure about how dark the color is, test on the fondant trimmings first.

Use a fine paintbrush dipped in **black food coloring** to paint tiny footprints in certain areas of the map. Write "Hogwarts" and any additional names or decorations you like.

TOP TIP

This is a free-form map, so you can make your own design. You can copy the design used in the photograph or create your own. You might want to practice drawing one using pencil and paper first. Remember to have several corridors on the map and another space to paint "Hogwarts."

HOGWARTS HOUSE SCARF CAKE

Are you brave like a Gryffindor, wise like a Ravenclaw, loyal like a Hufflepuff, or cunning like a Slytherin? You'll need to decide which Hogwarts house you belong to before you start this tempting cake. Or hedge your bets and make all four!

🕐 **1 HOUR** 🍴 **SERVES 12**

Vanilla Sponge Cake (approximately 10 x 8 inches/ 25.5 x 20 cm)

12 oz/350 g Buttercream Frosting

TO DECORATE

Red, green, yellow, or blue natural food coloring (see opposite)

3 oz/75 g red, green, yellow, or blue fondant (see opposite)

3½ oz/100 g yellow, gray, or black fondant (see opposite)

Confectioners'/icing sugar, for dusting

SPECIAL EQUIPMENT

Small spatula/palette knife

Cut your baked, cooled **cake** (see page 86) in half widthwise and place the pieces end to end to make a long, thin rectangle (see Top Tip).

TOP TIP

This cake needs to be assembled on a long board or tray. A long, thin cutting board is ideal. Don't worry if it's a little too short—you can always trim your cake to fit. If you don't have a board long enough, you can cut a piece of foam board to 17 × 7 inches/ 43 × 18 cm and cover it with foil instead.

2

Beat a few drops of your **food coloring** into the **buttercream** (see page 88) until you have your desired color. Spread a small amount of frosting between the ends of the two **cakes** and press them firmly together. Spread the remainder of the frosting all over the top and sides of the cake until it's covered in an even layer. Use a spatula to smooth the frosting as neatly as possible.

3

Roll out your chosen **fondant** color on a surface dusted with **confectioners' sugar** into a generous 5 × 2½ inch/12.5 × 6.5 cm rectangle. Trim off the edges of your rectangle to neaten and cut the rectangle in half lengthwise. Make deep cuts all along one long edge of one rectangle for the scarf's tassels. Lift into position so the uncut edge meets the **buttercream** at one end of the **cake**. Use your fingers to break up the tassels. Repeat this with the other rectangle of fondant for the opposite end of the cake.

4

Thinly roll out the chosen stripe **fondant** color to a 6½ × 4 inch/16.5 × 10 cm rectangle and cut lengthwise into ten thin strips. Lay two strips over the center of the cake, leaving a small space in between. Let the ends trail over the sides, trimming off any excess with scissors. Arrange four more double strips of fondant over the cake as shown in the photograph.

DID YOU KNOW?

You can make this Hogwarts House Scarf Cake in the colors of your favorite House. Our version is Hufflepuff, but you can also try Gryffindor, Ravenclaw, or Slytherin.

GRYFFINDOR

Use deep red food coloring for the frosting and red fondant for the tassels. Use yellow fondant for the stripes.

SLYTHERIN

Use green food coloring for the frosting and green fondant for the tassels. Use gray fondant for the stripes.

HUFFLEPUFF

Use yellow food coloring for the frosting and yellow fondant for the tassels. Use black fondant for the stripes.

RAVENCLAW

Use deep blue food coloring for the frosting and blue fondant for the tassels. Use gray fondant for the stripes.

HARRY'S BIRTHDAY CAKE

Harry's iconic eleventh birthday cake from the first film is easy to replicate—down to the cracked surface, caused when Hagrid accidentally sat on it! You can easily personalize this cake by swapping Harry's name for your own or the name of a friend or family member.

45 MINS **SERVES 10**

 2 Vanilla Sponge Cakes (approximately 10 inches/25.5 cm in diameter each)

 12 oz/350 g Buttercream Frosting

4 tbsp strawberry or raspberry jam

Pink and green natural food coloring

SPECIAL EQUIPMENT

Small paper or plastic piping bag

Small spatula/palette knife

Place one of the cooled, baked **cakes** (see pages 86–87) on a plate or board and spread the top with 4 tablespoons of the **buttercream** (see page 88). Spoon **jam** on top of the buttercream and spread to the edges. Position the second cake on top.

Transfer 3 tablespoons of the reserved buttercream to a small bowl and mix in a few drops of **green food coloring**. Transfer to a small piping bag. Set aside.

2

Mix enough **pink food coloring** into the remaining **buttercream** to color it deep pink. Using a small spatula, spread the buttercream as smoothly as possible over the top and sides of the cake until it's covered in an even layer.

3

Cut the smallest tip off the piping bag so the **green buttercream** can be piped in a thin line. Pipe "Happee Birthdae Harry" (or another name) onto the top of the cake.

TOP TIP

If you're unsure about how to space the letters on the cake, draw an 8 inch/20 cm circle on a sheet of paper and write out the birthday message. (You can use the cake tin or a plate as a guide for drawing the circle.) This will give you an idea of how big to pipe your letters.

MAGICAL FACT

Despite the fact that it arrived a little squashed, Hagrid's handmade birthday cake was extra special to Harry as it was the first one he'd ever been given! The kindly half-giant also gifted The Boy Who Lived his snowy owl, Hedwig.

4

Use the tip of a toothpick or wooden skewer to score the surface of the **cake** with a crack. See the photograph for the exact positioning.

HOGWARTS: A HISTORY CAKE

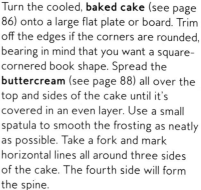

Written by Bathilda Bagshot, this essential textbook for all Hogwarts students might look dusty and musty but it's freshly baked and, of course, absolutely delicious. It would make a perfect birthday cake for any knowledgeable Harry Potter fan who loves to read—just like Hermione!

1½ HOURS **SERVES 12**

Vanilla Sponge Cake (approximately 10 x 8 inches/ 25 x 20 cm)

12 oz/350 g Chocolate Buttercream Frosting

7 oz/200 g dark brown fondant

Confectioners'/icing sugar, for dusting

3½ oz/100 g white fondant

Tube of gold decorator frosting/icing

Several lengths of red fruit leather or any other thick candy ribbons

1 thin rectangular wafer cookie/wafer, about 3½ x 1¾ inches/9 x 4.5 cm

Tube of brown or black decorator frosting/icing

SPECIAL EQUIPMENT

Small spatula/palette knife

Ruler

1

Turn the cooled, **baked cake** (see page 86) onto a large flat plate or board. Trim off the edges if the corners are rounded, bearing in mind that you want a square-cornered book shape. Spread the **buttercream** (see page 88) all over the top and sides of the cake until it's covered in an even layer. Use a small spatula to smooth the frosting as neatly as possible. Take a fork and mark horizontal lines all around three sides of the cake. The fourth side will form the spine.

2

Place the **brown fondant** on a surface dusted with **confectioners' sugar** and flatten. Break off pieces of **white fondant** and scatter them over the brown. Fold the fondant over and start kneading and squeezing it until it becomes marbled with color. Turn it in the sugar dusted surface as you go, sprinkling with more confectioners' sugar so it doesn't get too sticky. Once the fondant is marbled with patches of white, it is ready.

3

Measure the top of the cake and down over the spine with a ruler and add ¼ inch/5 mm to this. Jot the total down on a piece of paper so you don't forget. Roll out the **fondant** until slightly larger than this measurement. Trim off the edges to the size you've noted. Lift the fondant over the top of the cake and down the spine, trimming off any excess at the base. You might need to pull the edges of the fondant out a little as it can get misshapen during transfer. The book will look most effective if the fondant comes just over the edges of the buttercream.

4

Re-roll the brown fondant trimmings, cut out long strips about ¼ inch/5 mm wide, and position around the three remaining sides of the cake, trimming off the excess to fit. Trace and cut out the *Hogwarts: A History* Cake **template** on page 90.

TOP TIP

If you're not confident with piping letters, practice on a wafer cookie before positioning it on the cake. You might need a few attempts, but practice makes perfect!

5

Rest the template on top of the cake and pipe a line of **gold decorator frosting** around the castle shape, but not along the base. Carefully lift away the template. Position several lengths of **fruit leather** or **candy** down the left-hand side of the cake, trimming off the excess with scissors. Use dots of **decorator frosting** to hold it in place if necessary.

6

Position the **wafer cookie** near the lower edge of the cake. Write "Hogwarts" and "A History" in **brown or black decorator frosting**. Pipe a line of gold decorator frosting around the edges of the wafer.

MAGICAL FACT

In the first film, Hermione tells Ron and Harry that she breezed through *Hogwarts: A History* for a bit of "light reading"—before school even started!

CUPCAKES AND CAKE POPS

Forbidden Forest Fancies

Platform 9¾ Cupcakes

Dragon Egg Delights

Pumpkin Patch Cake

Pygmy Puffs

Golden Snitch Winged Wonders

Acromantula Cupcake Stack

Gringotts Dragon

Mimbulus Mimbletonia

Lollipop Cake Pops

FORBIDDEN FOREST FANCIES

The Forbidden Forest, which borders the edges of Hogwarts, is strictly off-limits to students. You'd think this might tempt a few of the more daring pupils to have a peek, but with rumors of Unicorns, Centaurs, and Acromantulas living inside, even the bravest aren't that foolhardy. This delicious replica is another matter entirely. You'll definitely break a few rules to get your hands on a bite!

1 HOUR — **SERVES 12**

7 oz/200 g Buttercream Frosting

Green natural food coloring

12 Vanilla Cupcakes, preferably in green and black paper liners

7 oz/200 g Chocolate Buttercream Frosting

½ cup/75 g dark chocolate chips

20 small rose leaves, rinsed and dried (see Top Tip)

3 soft black jelly candies/sweets

1 chunky licorice stick

6 miniature white candies/sweets

Tube of white decorator frosting/icing

4-6 tbsp chocolate sprinkles

Cocoa powder, for dusting

SPECIAL EQUIPMENT

Paintbrush, approximately ¼ inch/5 mm in diameter

Small paper or plastic piping bag

Small spatula or palette knife

Small sieve or tea strainer

1

Color the **buttercream frosting** (see page 88) with **green food coloring**. Spread over half the **cupcakes** (see pages 86-87) and fluff up the surface with a fork. Reserve 3 tablespoons of the **chocolate buttercream** and spread the rest over the remaining cupcakes. Melt the **chocolate chips** (see page 89).

2

Using a paintbrush, spread the **chocolate** over the undersides of the **rose leaves** until generously coated. Transfer to a small board or tray lined with parchment paper and chill until set. Meanwhile, transfer the remaining melted chocolate to a small piping bag and snip off the tip so the chocolate flows in a thin line. (If the chocolate has started to thicken before you put it in the bag, you can reheat it briefly using the same method you used for melting.)

3

Using a small spatula, spread the reserved **chocolate buttercream** over a large flat plate or board. Arrange the **cupcakes** in a similar position to those in the photograph.

4

Pipe the **chocolate** in the bag over the **green frosted cakes** to represent tree roots. Let the piping flow over the sides of the cupcakes and onto the board.

MAGICAL FACT

Rather than using CGI, the Harry Potter production team built a life-size model of Aragog. With Acromantulas capable of growing to the size of elephants, this meant that each of the creature's legs was six meters long.

5

To shape the spiders, place the soft **black jelly candies** on three of the **frosted cupcakes**. Cut the **licorice** into 1¼ inch/3 cm lengths. Slice these into very thin pieces, each smaller that a matchstick. Arrange four on either side of each jelly, curving them and pushing into the buttercream to secure in place for legs. Secure the miniature **white candies** in place with dots of **decorator frosting** for eyes.

6

Using your fingers, scatter the **chocolate sprinkles** all over the chocolate frosted cakes. Carefully peel the **rose petals** away from the chocolate. Arrange the chocolate leaves over the cakes, pushing some gently into the **cupcakes** and some onto the board.

7

Use the **white decorator frosting** to pipe a spiderweb shape onto the buttercream on the board. Place the **cocoa powder** in a small sieve or tea strainer and lightly dust over the cakes.

TOP TIP

The veining on rose leaves makes an impression in chocolate that looks very realistic once the chocolate sets. Herbs such as bay leaves can also be used for making chocolate leaves, but rose leaves are the most effective. Don't be tempted to use any other leaves from the garden!

PLATFORM 9 3/4 CUPCAKES

Practice your frosting and piping skills on these beautifully decorated cupcakes before they disappear—just like the young witches and wizards heading through Platform 9¾ to the Hogwarts Express! The brickwork piping might take a little practice. Pipe your bricks on a plate or board before you start decorating the real thing.

45-60 MINS | MAKES 12

- 12 oz/350 g Buttercream Frosting
- Red and brown natural food coloring

- 12 Vanilla Cupcakes, preferably in red, brown, or black paper liners
- 12 giant white chocolate discs/buttons
- Tube of black decorator frosting/icing

SPECIAL EQUIPMENT
Small spatula/palette knife
Paper or plastic piping bag
Small piping tube

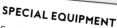

Spoon 2 heaped tablespoons of the **buttercream** (see page 88) into a separate bowl and reserve. Beat a few drops each of **red and brown food coloring** into the remainder of the frosting until it is a deep red brick color.

Place a spoonful on top of one **cupcake** (see pages 86–87). Using a small spatula, spread the frosting from the center to the paper liner so it's as smooth as possible all over. Repeat with the remainder of the cupcakes.

2

3

Cut about ½ inch/l cm off the tip of the piping bag and fit the piping tube into it. Place the reserved **buttercream** in the bag, twist the open end to seal the frosting in, and squeeze it to the tip. Pipe lines across each cupcake, about ½ inch/l cm apart. Pipe shorter lines in between to create a brick design.

Place an upturned **white chocolate disc** onto the center of a cupcake, pressing it down gently so the chocolate is held in place. Repeat with the remaining cupcakes.

TOP TIP
~ ★ ~

You can easily make your own white chocolate disc if you can't find any at the supermarket. Melt a little white chocolate in a bowl (see page 89). Line a small baking sheet or board with parchment paper. Take a scant half teaspoon of the chocolate and spoon it onto the paper. Spread with the back of the spoon until it's 1 inch/2.5 cm in diameter. Make more discs in the same way and chill for about 30 minutes before using.

4

Use the **black decorator frosting** to pipe "9¾" onto the chocolate discs. You might want to practice on a plate or napkin first.

MAGICAL FACT

In the second movie, Harry and Ron fly Arthur Weasley's Ford Anglia to Hogwarts after they are unable to get through the gateway to Platform 9¾. They later learn that the house-elf Dobby had prevented their access to try to save Harry from a threat at school.

DRAGON EGG DELIGHTS

One of the most heartwarming scenes in the first Harry Potter film is little Norbert the Norwegian Ridgeback hatching out of his shell. Of course, he then proceeds to set Hagrid's beard on fire, which isn't quite as cute! Re-create your own dragon eggs with this clever recipe. They're perfect for a special party, tea, or snack time.

⏱ 45 MINS   🔥 2-3 MIN   🍴 MAKES 6

3 cups/100 g crisped rice cereal

¼ stick/25 g butter

3 cups/150 g white, or pink and white mini marshmallows

½ cup/75 g milk chocolate chips

4 dark chocolate sandwich cookies/biscuits

5 tbsp milk chocolate curls

Multicolored sprinkles

SPECIAL EQUIPMENT

1 large paper or plastic bag

Paper liners, preferably dark brown or black

1 Line 6 sections of a muffin pan with paper liners. Put the **cereal** in a paper or plastic bag and crush lightly with a rolling pin to break into smaller pieces.

2 Melt the **butter** in a medium-sized saucepan, tip in the **marshmallows**, and heat very gently until the marshmallows have melted, stirring once or twice. This will take 2-3 minutes. Remove from the heat and pour in the **cereal**, reserving the bag. Mix well with a spoon and put the mixture into a bowl (see Top Tip). Be careful because the saucepan will be very hot.

3 Take a teaspoonful of the **mixture** and shape it into a small oval. Place the shape on your work surface and neaten into an egg shape. Make seventeen more in the same way. (And don't forget that dipping your fingers in cold water will stop the stickiness.)

4 Spoon the remaining **mixture** into the paper liners, pressing down gently with the back of a wet spoon. Melt the **chocolate chips** (see page 89). Use a teaspoon to drizzle the chocolate over the mixture in the liners.

Melt the **chocolate chips** (see page 89).

5 Crush the **sandwich cookies** in the reserved bag and sprinkle over the nests along with the **chocolate curls**.

6 Scatter the **sprinkles** onto a small plate and turn the eggs in them until partially coated. Arrange three eggs in each nest. Leave to set for about 30 minutes in the fridge or a cool place.

TOP TIP

✦ ★ ✦

Melted marshmallows are very sticky! You'll find this recipe much easier if you use cutlery (and fingers!) dipped in water when you transfer or shape the mixture. Have a little bowl of cold water next to you so you don't have to keep going to the sink.

MAGICAL FACT

After sweet Norwegian Ridgeback Norbert hatched in Hagrid's hut, he was sent to live in Romania with Ron's older brother Charlie who worked at a dragon sanctuary.

PUMPKIN PATCH CAKE

When it comes to growing vegetables, Hagrid has the magic touch (aided, as we discover in the second film, by flesh-eating slug repellent from Knockturn Alley). His pride and joy, of course, are the enormous pumpkins in his gamekeeper's garden. Try your hand at these cupcake-sized ones—they're far more manageable to hold and just as tasty.

 1-1½ HOURS   **SERVES 10-12**

 12 oz/350 g Buttercream Frosting

Green and orange natural food coloring

 12 Vanilla Cupcakes, preferably in orange paper liners

Tubes of orange and green decorator frosting/icing

Confectioners'/icing sugar, for dusting

Small piece of green fondant

½ cup/50 g shredded sweetened coconut

SPECIAL EQUIPMENT

Small spatula/palette knife

1 Transfer a quarter of the **buttercream** (see page 88) to a separate bowl and beat in a little **green food coloring**. Spread this onto a large rectangular board measuring at least 18 x 8 inches/46 x 20 cm, or similar.

2 Remove the paper liners from four of the **cupcakes** (see pages 86–87) and cut the cupcakes in half horizontally. (You will only need the bottom halves for this recipe.) Trim off the edges. These will form the smaller pumpkins that will be submerged in the grass.

3 Mix the remaining **buttercream** with a few drops of **orange food coloring** to make a deep orange color. Place a spoonful on top of one whole **cupcake**. Using a small spatula, spread the frosting from the center to the paper liner. Try to dome the frosting up in the center to create a rounded shape. Repeat with the remaining whole cupcakes, reserving a little of the frosting for the halved cupcakes.

4 Use the **orange decorator frosting** to pipe curved lines from one point at the edge of each whole cupcake to the opposite edge, as in the photograph.

> **TOP TIP**
> ❦☆❧
> If you can't get orange food coloring, use a mixture of red and yellow, adding a little to the buttercream at a time until you have a nice deep orange color.

Dust your fingers with a little **confectioners' sugar** and make cone shapes from the **green fondant**. Secure them to the pumpkins for stalks. Pipe a few green lines of **decorator frosting** out from the stalks.

5 Arrange the whole and halved **cupcakes** on the frosted board and spread the cupcake halves with the remaining **buttercream**. Pipe orange lines from the center of the halved cupcakes down to the board.

7 Put the **shredded coconut** in a bowl with a little **green food coloring** and mix with a teaspoon until the coconut is colored. Spoon around the pumpkins to complete the grass.

47

PYGMY PUFFS

Miniature Puffskeins are cute little creatures sold at Weasleys' Wizard Wheezes. Ginny gets a pink one as a pet in the sixth film. These cupcake versions are almost as adorable. Take your time spreading and peaking the butter-cream frosting on top of the cakes to give the Pygmy Puffs their characteristic fluffiness.

1 HOUR   **SERVES 12**

Pink natural food coloring

12 oz/350 g Buttercream Frosting

12 Vanilla Cupcakes, preferably in pink paper liners

24 round mint candies/sweets, about ¾ inch/2 cm in diameter

24 milk chocolate chips

Black or dark red fruit lace

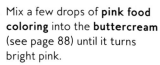

Mix a few drops of **pink food coloring** into the **buttercream** (see page 88) until it turns bright pink.

MAGICAL FACT

In the sixth movie we learn, courtesy of Luna Lovegood, that Pygmy Puffs sing on Boxing Day (a holiday in the UK that falls on the day after Christmas).

2

Place a spoonful of **frosting** on top of one **cupcake** (see pages 86–87) and spread roughly to the edges. Using the tip of a fork, fluff up the frosting all over the surface to resemble the Pygmy Puff's fur. The more you do this, the fluffier it will become! Repeat with the remainder and reserve the scrapings in the bowl.

3

Position two **mint candies** toward one edge of each cupcake so they're almost touching. Dot the smallest amount of **buttercream** left in the bowl on the base of the **chocolate chips** and position on the centers of the mints.

TOP TIP

The lighter and creamier your buttercream frosting, the easier it will be to shape into fluffy peaks on the cupcakes. The flavor will be better too!

4

Cut very short lengths of **fruit lace**, about ½ inch/l cm long. Bend a piece into a curve and position just below the eyes for the mouth.

GOLDEN SNITCH WINGED WONDERS

Everyone will want to catch one of these delicious Quidditch-themed treats. Made of tasty vanilla cake, white chocolate, and lemon, they're golden little nuggets of flavor on the inside and outside! You'll need a little patience as they need several stages of chilling—as well as two days for the wings to set—but they're well worth the wait!

 1½–2 HOURS, PLUS CHILLING AND SETTING **MAKES 8**

TO DECORATE
Confectioners'/icing sugar, for dusting

3 oz/75 g ivory/white fondant

1 cup/150 g white chocolate chips

Edible gold food spray

FOR THE CAKE POP
 6 oz/175 g Vanilla Sponge Cake (see Top Tip)

Finely grated zest of 1 lemon, plus 2 tsp juice

2 tbsp confectioners'/icing sugar

¼ cup/40 g white chocolate chips

SPECIAL EQUIPMENT
Two 2 inch/5 cm diameter cardboard tubes, such as those from a paper towel/kitchen roll or kitchen foil, wrapped in parchment paper and secured with tape to a tray or board to hold in place (see step 1)

8 cake pop sticks or wooden lollipop sticks

Make the wings 48 hours before the cake pops. Trace and cut out the Snitch wings **templates** on page 90. On a surface dusted with **confectioners' sugar**, thinly roll out the **fondant**. Place the templates over the fondant and cut out a pair of wings using a small knife. Use the tip of the knife to score the wing markings as on the template. Gently rest the shapes over the tubes to set. Be sure to angle the wings over the tube so they're not too tightly curled. Make seven more sets of wings in the same way. (You might like to make a few spares, too.) Leave to set for 48 hours uncovered, in a dry place. Don't refrigerate.

TOP TIP Use any bought or homemade vanilla sponge cake to create these cake pops. If you make the Vanilla Sponge Cake recipe on page 86, bake it in any shape you like—you only need the crumbs for this recipe! However, cupcakes are ideal. You'll only need about 4 cupcakes for the cake pop crumbs, so you can use the remainder for another cupcake recipe or simply spread with frosting and enjoy!

2

To make the cake pop filling, crumble the **sponge cake** (see page 86) into a bowl. Add the **lemon zest** and **juice**. Stir in the **confectioners' sugar**. Melt the **chocolate chips** (see page 89) and add the melted chocolate to the bowl. Mix together until you have a thick paste. Form the mixture into a ball and tip it out onto your work surface.

3

Cut into eight even-sized wedges and shape each into a ball in the palms of your hands. Place the balls on a small board or tray lined with parchment paper and chill for at least 1 hour.

4

Melt the **white chocolate** for decorating (see page 89). Dip ½ inch/1 cm of the end of a cake pop stick into the melted chocolate and push it into the center of a cake pop ball. Repeat with the remainder and chill for another 10 minutes.

7

Spray the cake pops with **gold spray**. Store in the fridge or in a cool place.

5

Hold a cake pop over the bowl of **melted chocolate** and use a teaspoon to drizzle the chocolate over the cake until it is completely covered, twisting the stick as you work. The chocolate doesn't need to be perfectly smooth—the Golden Snitch isn't smooth either! Return the cake pops to the fridge for at least 15 minutes before adding the wings.

6

Re-melt the **chocolate** if it has set around the sides of the bowl. Spoon a very small amount of the chocolate onto the edge of a **fondant wing** as shown on the **templates**. Gently press the wing against one side of the cake pop and hold for about 30 seconds until it sets in place. Secure another wing on the other side and then repeat with the remaining cake pops.

TOP TIP
~∞☆∞~

Inexpensive cake pop stands are an easy way of serving your cake pops and will also support them while you add decorations. As an alternative, use a large bowl filled with sugar or push the sticks into a halved melon or squash, inverted onto a plate.

ACROMANTULA CUPCAKE STACK

It's no wonder poor Ron is deathly scared of spiders—he and Harry barely escape from the fearsome Aragog and his hordes of hungry children in the second film. But this deliciously chocolately cupcake version of the 15-foot Acromantula is pure fun to assemble and a treat for the tastebuds.

1–1½ HOURS | **SERVES 11**

- ¼ stick/25 g unsalted butter, softened
- ⅓ cup/40 g confectioners'/icing sugar
- 12 oz/350 g Chocolate Buttercream Frosting
- 11 Brownie Cupcakes, preferably in brown or black paper liners
- 1 chocolate cookie/biscuit about 2¾ inches/7 cm in diameter
- 2 large chocolate-coated candies/sweets
- 8 thick sticks of licorice, at least 4½–5 inches/11.5–13 cm long
- 4 mini chocolate candies/sweets

SPECIAL EQUIPMENT
Small paper or plastic piping bag

Beat together the **butter** and **sugar** until smooth and creamy. Beat in a tablespoon of the **chocolate buttercream** (see page 88) and place in a paper or plastic piping bag. Set aside for piping the features.

Place a double stack of 8 **brownie cupcakes** (see page 85), all still in their liners, on a flat plate or board in the formation shown, using a small blob of **buttercream** to secure the top layer to the lower layer.

3

Using a small, round-bladed knife, spread another **cupcake** with a little **buttercream**. Cut the **cookie** in half and arrange it on top of the cupcake so the straight sides face outward. Spread the cookie with more buttercream to cover. Position two **chocolate-coated candies** on top for the eyes.

4

Spread the top of the **cupcake** stack with **buttercream** as well as the exposed edges of the bottom layer of cupcakes. Place the remaining cupcakes on the center of the stack and spread with more buttercream. Rest the spider's face cupcake in front, letting it tilt at an angle against the uppermost cupcake.

5

For the legs, cut four **licorice sticks** in half lengthwise. If they are very thick, you could cut them smaller into quarters instead. Rest four licorice lengths up against each side of the stack so the tops rest against the tops of the liners.

6

Halve the remaining sticks of **licorice** and cut into 1¾ inch/4.5 cm lengths. Rest these over the cupcakes, meeting the longer lengths of licorice to form the tops of the legs.

7

TOP TIP

For a special occasion you could always add some individual little spider cupcakes around the Giant Acromantula for Aragog's children.

Snip off the tip of the piping bag so the **frosting** can be piped in a thin line. Use the bag to pipe the facial features of the spider as shown in the photograph. Arrange the four mini **chocolate candies** in a row under the eyes. Pipe further decorative lines onto the legs and along the back.

GRINGOTTS DRAGON

The dragon found below Gringotts Wizarding Bank is the palest of the dragons in the Harry Potter films. Its color, or lack of it, is due to the beast being kept underground until Harry, Ron, and Hermione help it escape. This is one of the easiest decorations in the book, but still visually effective, and much cuter than the fearsome real thing!

🕐 **1 HOUR** | 🍴🍽️ **SERVES 12**

- 12 Vanilla Cupcakes
- 12 oz/350 g Buttercream Frosting
- Several giant white marshmallows
- 2 large soft jelly candies/sweets in black, red, or green
- 2 small candy-coated chocolates, any color
- 2 chunky chocolate chew candies/sweets or fudge pieces
- 2 fan-shaped ice-cream wafers or graham crackers

Arrange nine of the **cupcakes** (see pages 86–87) on a large board in the position shown in the photograph. Make all the cupcakes touch and place the ones at the back in a curve to shape the tail.

TOP TIP

By adding a little food coloring to the buttercream, you can create one of the other Harry Potter dragons. How about a brownish red for the Norwegian Ridgeback, a brighter red for the Chinese Fireball, or a light green for the Common Welsh Green?

2

Unwrap the remaining three **cupcakes**. Cut two of these in half and position on either side of the thick body section for the limbs. Have the bases of these halves facing forward. Cut the remaining cupcake into two pieces so one piece is larger than the other. Arrange these for the tail end.

3

Spread the **buttercream** (see page 88) over the head, body, and tail using a round-bladed knife. Use more buttercream to cover the four limb pieces. You might find it easier to lift each cupcake, spread with frosting, and then replace where it was. Use the remainder of the frosting to spread over the spaces in between the cupcakes so you can't see where they meet.

4

Halve one giant **marshmallow** for eyes, adding two soft **jelly candies** for the centers. Secure these in place with a scraping of **buttercream** left in the bowl. Attach the **candy-coated chocolates** on the front cupcake for nostrils. Cut triangular pieces from the **chocolate chews** and secure in front of the limbs for claws.

5

Cut slices from more **marshmallows** then cut in half again to make semicircles. Position these along the back and tail of the dragon. Gently push the **fan wafers** or **graham crackers** into the body for the wings.

MIMBULUS MIMBLETONIA

Unlike the rare and magical *Mimbulus mimbletonia* plant (which releases a disgusting substance called Stinksap when it's prodded), this recipe looks, smells, and tastes delicious! The cupcakes are all chocolate flavored, but there's a choice of toppings, from crunchy pretzel sticks to chewy candies, so you can customize your creation!

1 HOUR   **SERVES 12**

- 12 Chocolate Cupcakes
- 12 oz/350g Buttercream Frosting
- 1½ tbsp cocoa powder
- Green natural food coloring
- 8 doughnut holes/mini doughnuts or small round chocolate truffles
- 6–8 chocolate finger cookies/biscuits or chocolate-coated pretzel sticks
- 3 brown or purple chocolate candies/sweets
- 8–10 red gummies/gums or soft candies/sweets
- 2 thick, long candy rolls or thick candy laces
- 1 tbsp small red candies/sweets or sprinkles
- 8–10 mini yellow chocolate-covered candies/sweets
- Tube of yellow decorator frosting/icing

TOP TIP

If making your own cupcakes, you might want to bake three of the cupcakes in brown paper liners for the flowerpot part of the cake.

1

Place three **cupcakes** (see pages 86–87) in a triangle at one end of a rectangular board. This will form the flowerpot. Arrange the remaining cupcakes above the flowerpot cupcakes in the squiggly shape of the plant. You might need to reposition the arrangement so it fits centrally on the board.

Transfer a quarter of the **buttercream** (see page 88) to a separate bowl and beat in the **cocoa powder** and 1 teaspoon hot water. Using a round-bladed knife, spread the chocolate buttercream over the three cupcakes at the base to roughly shape a flowerpot.

Mix a little **green food coloring** into the remaining **buttercream** until it becomes pale green. Spread over the remaining **cupcakes** right to the edges, but don't worry about making it too neat—the *Mimbulus mimbletonia* isn't! Spread the remaining green buttercream over the **doughnuts** and position as you like over the green cupcakes.

Use the **chocolate finger cookies or chocolate-covered pretzel sticks** to decorate the flowerpot as shown in the photograph. You'll need to break the cookies for the center decoration or add extra pieces for the longer lengths. Position three **brown or purple candies** to decorate.

Use the **red candies** to decorate the green frosted **cakes**. For the spikes, use scissors to snip the **candy rolls or laces** into triangles and position. Scatter with **red candies or sprinkles**. Secure the small **yellow candies** onto the **red gummies** with a dot of **yellow decorator frosting**. Pipe pointy tips onto the spikes.

MAGICAL FACT

Neville Longbottom became a brilliant Herbology student during his time at Hogwarts, even managing to keep up with Hermione's intellect during these lessons!

LOLLIPOP CAKE POPS

These tasty little bites mimic the colorful giant lollipops served at feasts in Hogwarts's Great Hall. They're easy to make, but they do need a little chilling and setting at various stages, so you won't be able to try them right away. But, trust us, they're well worth the wait!

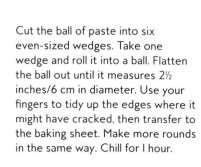

1 HOUR, PLUS CHILLING AND SETTING

MAKES 6

8 oz/225 g Vanilla Sponge Cake (approximately 3-4 cupcakes or a small sponge cake)

¼ cup/40 g milk chocolate chips

½ tsp strawberry or orange extract

2 tbsp confectioners'/icing sugar

7 oz/200 g Royal Icing

Pink and black natural food coloring

SPECIAL EQUIPMENT

6 cake pop sticks or wooden lollipop sticks

Small paper or plastic piping bag

Wire cooling rack

1

Line a baking sheet with parchment paper. To make the cake pops, crumble the **cake** (see page 86) into a bowl. Melt the **chocolate chips** (see page 89) and add to the bowl with the **strawberry or orange extract** and **confectioners' sugar**. Mix the ingredients together until they are thoroughly combined and you have a thick paste. Shape the mixture into a ball and turn it out onto your work surface.

2

Cut the ball of paste into six even-sized wedges. Take one wedge and roll it into a ball. Flatten the ball out until it measures 2½ inches/6 cm in diameter. Use your fingers to tidy up the edges where it might have cracked, then transfer to the baking sheet. Make more rounds in the same way. Chill for 1 hour.

3 Push a cake pop or lollipop stick horizontally into each **cake pop**. Make sure you push it right through to the center and keep the stick horizontal so it doesn't poke through the side of the dough. Chill for an additional 10 minutes.

4 Transfer a quarter of the **royal icing** (see page 89) to a small bowl. Stir in a few drops of **pink food coloring** so it matches the color in the photograph. Spoon into a small paper or plastic piping bag. Add a few drops of cold water to the remaining icing to thin its consistency slightly—it should thickly coat the back of a spoon.

5 Place a cooling rack over a sheet of parchment paper on another baking sheet, or the one you used before and space the **cake pops** on the rack. Spoon the **white icing** over each cake pop and spread to the edges with the back of a spoon. The excess will run onto the parchment paper.

7 Once the white icing has stopped dripping onto the parchment, carefully transfer the cake pops to a clean sheet of parchment paper and leave to set completely for several hours. Once the surface is dry to the touch, they can be stored flat and loosely covered with plastic film for several days.

6 Cut the very tip off the piping bag so the **pink icing** flows out in a thin line. Start at the center of a **cake pop** and pipe a squiggly line out to the edge, making the line thicker as you approach the edge. Pipe 5-6 more squiggly lines out to the edges to complete the pattern. Repeat on the remainder of the cake pops.

TOP TIP If the white icing doesn't run all over the sides of the pops, you can spread it gently with a pastry brush.

COOKIES AND BROWNIES

Sorting Hat Brownies

Hogwarts Crest Cookies

Great Hall Christmas Tree Cookies

Hogwarts Stained-Glass Windows

Wizard Chess Board Brownies

Chocolate Frog Hoppers

Fawkes the Phoenix Cookies

Hagrid's Hut Gingerbread Cookies

Quidditch Cookies

Hogsmeade Winter Warmers

SORTING HAT BROWNIES

The soft, gooey consistency of a chocolate brownie is perfect for molding and shaping into these little Sorting Hats. Be warned: it might get a little messy. But it's great fun to play around with expressions. Will your hats be decisive, conflicted, deep in thought—or all three? Let the "Sorting" begin!

45-60 MINS | **MAKES 12**

Chocolate Brownie (approximately 9 inches/23 cm square)

12 chocolate cookies/biscuits or chocolate coated cookies/biscuits, 2½-2¾ inch/6.5-7 cm in diameter

3 each of red, green, yellow, and blue candies/sweets

¼ cup/40 g plain chocolate chips

Use a knife to cut the pan of baked, cooled **brownies** (see page 85) into four even-sized long rectangles.

Make two cuts across in the opposite direction so that you end up with 12 pieces of brownie.

Use the yellow dotted lines as a cutting guide.

MAGICAL FACT

The Sorting Hat we see in the films was voiced by the late British actor Leslie Phillips. It was created using a combination of a real prop and clever special effects.

2

Take one piece of **brownie** and use your hands to mold it into a round cone shape with a pointy top. The base of the shape needs to be about 2 inches/5 cm in diameter so that it can be positioned on a cookie, leaving a rim around the edges.

3

Carefully push one **candy** into the base of each shaped brownie so that it is just hidden inside.

TOP TIP

If you buy premade brownie bites or bars, each one might be a little small for shaping in this recipe. If so, you may need to use more than one for each Sorting Hat. As a guide, each Sorting Hat should weigh about 2½ oz/65 g.

4

Once you form this basic shape, add creases in the sides to create the bends and folds in the Sorting Hat. Use a piece of cutlery such as a thick teaspoon handle to push mouth and eye cavities into the **brownie** near the base. If you're not happy with the shape, smooth it out and try again.

5

Bend the pointed top of the **brownie** over to complete the shape. Melt the **chocolate chips** in a small bowl. Place about ½ teaspoon of melted chocolate onto a **cookie** and position the brownie on top so a small rim shows around the edges. Repeat with the remaining brownies.

HOGWARTS CREST COOKIES

Show off your decorating skills with these clever little cookies, proudly presenting the four House colors: red for Gryffindor, green for Slytherin, yellow for Hufflepuff, and blue for Ravenclaw. These cookies are delicious no matter what House you're sorted into! Keep the cookies from softening by storing them in a shallow, airtight container. But don't stack them until the icing has set completely to avoid sticking and smearing.

🕐 1-2 HOURS, PLUS SETTING	🔥 15 MINS	🍴🍽️🔪 MAKES 7-8

 10 oz/300 g Sugar Cookie/Biscuit Dough

Tube of gold decorator frosting/icing

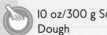 7 oz/200 g Royal Icing

Red, green, yellow, and blue natural food coloring

Tube of black decorator frosting/icing

SPECIAL EQUIPMENT
4 small paper or plastic piping bags

1

Line a baking sheet with parchment paper. Trace and cut out the two Hogwarts Crest Cookies **templates** on page 91. Thinly roll out the **dough** (see page 84) on a lightly floured surface and cut around the larger template. Transfer to the baking sheet and shape more cookies in the same way, cutting out shapes from the smaller template as well. Re-roll the trimmings and cut out more shapes, making sure you have the same amount of both. Chill for 30 minutes. Preheat the oven to 375°F/190°C/gas mark 5.

2

Bake the **cookies** for 15 minutes, until golden around the edges. Leave to cool on the baking sheet, then transfer to a board or plate. Once completely cooled, pipe a line of **gold decorator frosting** around the edges of the cookies as shown in the photograph. Pipe a cross in the center to divide the cookies into four sections.

3

Divide the **royal icing** (see page 89) among four small bowls. Use teacups or small mugs if you don't have enough bowls. Stir a few drops of one **food coloring** into each bowl. Add a drop of water to each bowl if necessary to thin out the consistency. You want the frosting to have a smooth, level surface when it's left to stand for a few seconds (see Top Tip). Spoon the frostings into four piping bags and snip a very small tip off the ends. Pipe the frostings, one at a time, into the sections of the cookies, making sure each color is in the right section. Squeeze the frosting almost to the **gold piping**. It should spread out to the edges because of its loose consistency.

4

TOP TIP

When thinning Royal Icing, you need the smallest amount of cold water. Just add one drop at a time until the icing loses its shape but isn't quite liquid when the spoon is lifted from the bowl.

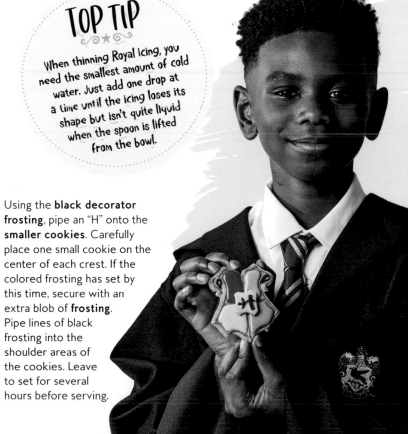

Using the **black decorator frosting**, pipe an "H" onto the **smaller cookies**. Carefully place one small cookie on the center of each crest. If the colored frosting has set by this time, secure with an extra blob of **frosting**. Pipe lines of black frosting into the shoulder areas of the cookies. Leave to set for several hours before serving.

GREAT HALL CHRISTMAS TREE COOKIES

Nowhere looks more stunning at Christmastime than the Great Hall at Hogwarts School of Witchcraft and Wizardry. These clever cookies are made using ice-cream cones for the trees and filled with little candies for an extra festive surprise!

1–1½ HOURS   **15 MINS**   **MAKES 8**

- 14 oz/400 g Gingerbread Cookie/ Biscuit Dough
- Green natural food coloring

- 12 oz/350 g Buttercream Frosting
- Approximately 1 cup/150 g small chocolate or chewy fruit candies/ sweets
- 8 pointed ice-cream cones
- Small edible gold stars
- Mini white marshmallows
- Tubes of orange and white decorator frosting/icing

SPECIAL EQUIPMENT

3 inch/7.5 cm round cookie cutter

Large paper or plastic piping bag

¼ inch/5 mm star piping tube

Preheat the oven to 375°F/190°C/gas mark 5. Line a baking sheet with parchment paper. Thinly roll out the **cookie dough** (see page 84) on a lightly floured surface. Cut out eight circles using the round cookie cutter and transfer them to the baking sheet. Re-roll the trimmings to make extra cookies. Bake for 15 minutes until golden. Leave to cool on the baking sheet.

2

Mix a few drops of **green food coloring** into the **buttercream** (see page 88). Once you're happy with the color, place the frosting in a large piping bag fitted with a ¼ inch/6 mm star piping tube.

3

Place some **small candies** in an **ice-cream cone** and pipe a little **buttercream** around the edge. Place one of the **cookies** on top so the buttercream seals the cone in place. Turn onto a board and make the remainder in the same way.

MAGICAL FACT

Every year, Hogwarts's Great Hall is decorated with twelve giant fir trees, covered in spectacular decorations! Hagrid helps to bring the giant trees from outside.

4

Pipe the **buttercream** around the **cone**. Pull the bag away slightly as you pipe to make the shapes a little longer. Continue to pipe the frosting up the cone, making the blobs smaller as you go, until it's completely covered. Repeat with the remainder.

5

TOP TIP
★ ★ ★

If you would like a more colorful Christmas tree decoration, swap the marshmallow candles for colorful mini candies. Alternatively cut out or mold small shapes in colored fondant.

Arrange plenty of **gold stars** over each tree. Arrange **mini marshmallows** in between. Pipe tiny "flames" at the top end of each marshmallow using **orange decorator frosting** to resemble lit candles. Pipe dots of **white decorator frosting** for snow.

HOGWARTS STAINED-GLASS WINDOWS

These cookies are inspired by the beautiful window in the prefects' bathroom, located on the fifth floor of Hogwarts (and available only to prefects). Melted hard candies are what give these treats their stunning stained-glass effect. And if you're feeling particularly adventurous, you can even try adding a mermaid. Just keep your fingers crossed Moaning Myrtle doesn't show up and ruin your fun!

🕐 1-1½ HOURS   🔥 13 MINS   🍽 MAKES 6

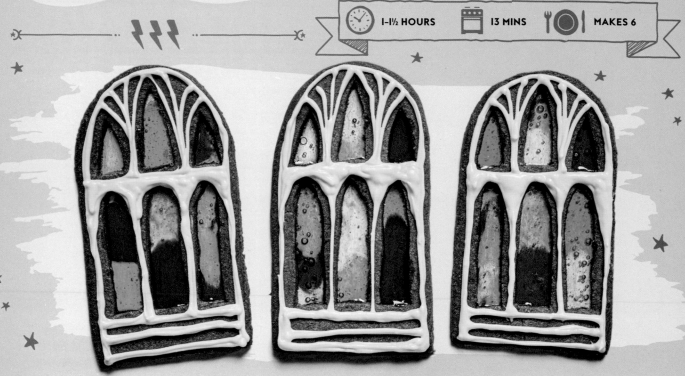

 14 oz/400 g Gingerbread Cookie/Biscuit Dough

18-20 multicolored hard candies/boiled sweets

½ cup/75 g white chocolate chips

SPECIAL EQUIPMENT

Large paper or plastic bag

Small paper or plastic piping bag

1

Line a baking sheet with parchment paper. Trace and cut out the Hogwarts Stained-Glass Windows **template** on page 92. Thinly roll out the **dough** (see page 84) on a lightly floured surface and cut around the outside of the template. Carefully lift the windows to the baking sheet. You should have enough dough for six cookies.

2

Cut out the six window sections, making sure you cut right into the corners. Carefully lift out these pieces of **dough**. You might be able to make one or two more cookies from the dough trimmings, but if you do, you'll need extra candies and chocolate for decorating. Chill the cookies while you prepare the candies and preheat the oven to 375°F/190°C/gas mark 5.

3

Unwrap the **candies** and space slightly apart in a large paper or plastic bag. Tap each cookie firmly with the end of a rolling pin to break into smaller pieces. Bake the cookies for 8 minutes.

4

Use your fingers to arrange the **candy** pieces into the spaces within the **cookies**. Take care not to touch the baking sheet as it will be hot. Return to the oven for about 5 minutes until the candies have melted to fill the spaces. Leave to cool on the baking sheet.

TOP TIP

Don't like gingerbread? This recipe works just as well with Sugar Cookie Dough, in which case you might prefer to use milk chocolate instead of white for the decoration to contrast with the window frames!

Melt the **chocolate** (see page 89). Place in a paper or plastic piping bag. Snip off a small tip from the bag so the chocolate flows out in a thin line. Use the chocolate to pipe over the **cookies** as shown in the photograph. You might want to practice on a piece of paper first. Leave to set in a cool place for at least 30 minutes before serving.

5

WIZARD CHESS BOARD BROWNIES

If, like Ron Weasley, you love chess and chocolate, then you're in for a treat with this recipe. A simplified version of the giant chessboard seen in the movies, these little brownies are topped with delicious chocolate spread and squares of yummy dark and white chocolate. As with any chocolate creation, this one is best decorated in a cool kitchen. If the chocolate starts to soften while you're decorating, simply pop it all back in the fridge for a little while. Altogether now: "Knight to H3!"

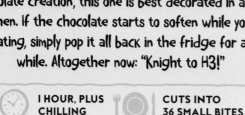

1 HOUR, PLUS CHILLING

CUTS INTO 36 SMALL BITES

¾ cup/115 g white chocolate chips

¾ cup/115g dark chocolate chips

Chocolate Brownie (approximately 9 inches/23 cm square)

5 tbsp chocolate hazelnut spread

Ivory/white and dark gray fondant (optional)

SPECIAL EQUIPMENT
Ruler
Small spatula/palette knife

Place the **white and dark chocolate chips** in two separate bowls and melt (see page 89). Using a ruler, draw two 9 x 4½ inch/23 x 11.5 cm rectangles onto separate pieces of parchment paper. Place on a baking sheet or tray. Scrape the white chocolate out of the bowl onto one piece and spread it carefully right to the edges with a back of a teaspoon. Tip the dark chocolate into the other rectangle and spread to the edges in the same way. Chill for at least 45 minutes.

MAGICAL FACT

The Sorcerer's Stone is guarded by a giant Wizard Chess Board in *Harry Potter and the Sorcerer's Stone* (or *Harry Potter and the Philosopher's Stone*, as it's called in the UK). Luckily, Ron is a skilled Wizard Chess player and guides his friends successfully across the game board.

DID YOU KNOW?

A real chessboard has 64 squares—that's eight rows of eight squares. If you want your brownie version to be more realistic, cut 32 smaller squares from each chocolate rectangle in step 3 instead. To do this, cut the chocolate into four even sized strips, then across to make 1 inch/3 cm squares.

Trim off the tiniest edge from each of the **chocolate rectangles** if they are not quite straight. (Don't trim off too much or your squares won't be big enough.) Cut each rectangle into three even-sized strips in a lengthways direction. Cut across the strips in the opposite direction to make small squares. As a rough guide each square should be a scant 1½ inches/4 cm, but don't worry too much as you can easily trim them down a little if they don't fit! Return the chocolate to the fridge if necessary, to firm up.

2

Carefully turn the cooled, baked **brownie** (see page 85) onto a flat plate or board. Spread with the **chocolate hazelnut spread** using a small spatula.

3

4

Carefully lift a square from the paper and place onto one corner of the **brownie**. You might find it easier to lift the square from the paper by sliding the clean spatula underneath. Gradually add the remaining squares, alternating the colors to create a simplified chessboard pattern. Store in a cool place until ready to serve.

And if you do actually use the board to play chess, you can eat your opponent's chess pieces when you win them! →

TOP TIP
⌁ ★ ⌁

Get creative by molding chessboard pieces in the same way you might use modeling clay. Use ivory and dark gray fondant and mold pieces using between ½–1 oz/12–25 g fondant for each piece. Secure each piece onto a small square base, about ¼ inch/5 mm deep. Shape small features like swords and crooks from more pieces of fondant and secure in place with a dampened paintbrush.

CHOCOLATE FROG HOPPERS

Of all the weird and wonderful candies Harry encounters during his very first train journey to Hogwarts, it's the Chocolate Frog that sticks out. (It's not every day your snack hops away, after all!) Just like The Boy Who Lived's escaping treat from the film, these little cookie delights will be gone before you know it.

| 🕐 **1½–2 HOURS PLUS CHILLING** | 🔥 **15 MINS** | 🍴 **MAKES 8** |

 10 oz/300 g Chocolate-Flavored Sugar Cookie/Biscuit Dough

½ cup/75 g milk chocolate chips

Confectioners'/icing sugar, for dusting

4½ oz/125 g purple fondant

3 oz/75 g chocolate-flavored fondant (see Top Tip)

16 mini colored candies/sweets

SPECIAL EQUIPMENT
Small paper or plastic piping bag

Line a baking sheet with parchment paper. Trace and cut out the Chocolate Frog Hoppers **template** on page 90. On a lightly floured surface, thinly roll out the **dough** (see page 84) and cut around the template. Transfer to the baking sheet. Shape more cookies in the same way, re-rolling the trimmings if necessary until you have eight cookies. Chill for 30 minutes. Preheat the oven to 375°F/190°C/gas mark 5.

MAGICAL FACT

Every chocolate frog comes with a collectable card featuring a famous witch or wizard. In *Harry Potter and the Sorcerer's Stone*, Ron boasts that he has about 500 Chocolate Frog cards!

TOP TIP
Don't worry if you can't get chocolate fondant. As an alternate, you can simply knead cocoa powder into white fondant until it's a rich brown color.

Bake the **cookies** for 15 minutes and leave to cool on the baking sheet. Melt the **chocolate chips** (see page 89). Cut the **template** along the dotted lines to make it slightly smaller.

On a surface dusted with **confectioners' sugar**, thinly roll out the **purple fondant** and cut around the template. Spread a dot of melted chocolate onto the center of each cookie and position the fondant on top, pressing down gently.

Shape the **chocolate fondant** into a ball, flatten it down on the surface, and cut into eight even-sized wedges. Roll each into an oval shape in the palms of your hands and then flatten one down on the center of each **cookie**.

Place the remaining **melted chocolate** in a paper or plastic piping bag. Snip off the tip so the chocolate can be piped in a thick line. Pipe limbs onto each cookie as in the photograph. To make the limbs thicker, particularly near the body, simply pipe more lines on top of the first.

Pipe a line of **chocolate** down the center of the backs and add a few dots on either side. Place two **mini colored candies** on each frog for eyes, securing in place with a dot of chocolate from the piping bag.

Add a small dot of **chocolate** to the center of each eye. Leave to set in a cool place for at least 30 minutes before serving.

FAWKES THE PHOENIX COOKIES

Create your own version of Albus Dumbledore's colorful creature companion with these delicious cookies. The topping is mostly buttercream, which remains soft, so don't stack your finished bakes. Instead, place in a shallow container such as a roasting tin or tray with sides and cover with plastic wrap. And don't worry—unlike Fawkes, at no point will these sweet treats burst into flames!

1½-2 HOURS PLUS CHILLING   **15 MINS**   **MAKES 8**

 10 oz/300 g Sugar Cookie/Biscuit Dough

Red natural food coloring

 7 oz/200 g Buttercream Frosting

Confectioners'/icing sugar, for dusting

2 oz/50 g yellow fondant

8 chocolate-coated pretzel sticks or chocolate finger cookies/biscuits (approximately 1½ inch/4 cm long)

Handful of soft chocolate chews or toffees

Tubes of red and black decorator frosting/icing

Line a baking sheet with parchment paper. Trace and cut out the Fawkes Cookies **template** on page 92. Thinly roll out the **dough** (see page 84) on a lightly floured surface and cut around the template. Transfer to the baking sheet, then shape more cookies in the same way. Re-roll the trimmings as needed to cut out eight cookies. Chill for 30 minutes. Preheat the oven to 375°F/190°C/gas mark 5.

MAGICAL FACT

A clever mix of CGI and a real puppet with colorful feathers brought Fawkes to life in the Harry Potter films. The puppet was so life-like, Dumbledore actor, the late Richard Harris, thought it was a real bird!

2

Bake the **cookies** for 15 minutes until golden around the edges. Leave to cool on the baking sheet. Mix a few drops of **red food coloring** into the **buttercream** (see page 88). Use a small, round-bladed knife to spread the frosting over the cookies. Use a fork to fluff up the frosting to resemble feathers.

3

Cut along the dotted lines of the **template** to remove the face and chest pieces. On a surface dusted with **confectioners' sugar**, thinly roll out the **yellow fondant**. Cut around the larger template and secure it to the chest area of each cookie by pressing down gently. Cut around the smaller template and secure it to the face. Repeat with the remainder.

4

Secure the **chocolate pretzel sticks** in place, pressing them gently into the buttercream. Cut slices from the **chocolate chews** and flatten if necessary to make ½ inch/1 cm squares. Press the outer edge of a small, round-bladed knife into the pieces to shape the claws.

5

Scribble the **red decorator frosting** over the ends of the wing, tail, and head feathers. You can smudge the decorator frosting into the **buttercream** a little with the tip of the piping tube. Use **black decorator frosting** to pipe the beaks and eyes.

DID YOU KNOW?

The phoenix is an immortal bird that obtains new life by rising from its own ashes. This happened to Fawkes in the second film when he burst into flames in front of Harry!

HAGRID'S HUT
GINGERBREAD COOKIES

Hagrid isn't known for his baking skills, but even the gentle half-giant couldn't go wrong with these cute little hut cookies, as all they require is a bit of patience and a steady hand. So if you're in the mood for something very tasty indeed, gather the ingredients below and enjoy creating eight mini masterpieces.

🕐 **1½–2 HOURS PLUS CHILLING**   🔥 **15 MINS**   🍽 **MAKES 8**

14 oz/400 g Gingerbread Cookie/Biscuit Dough

7 oz/200 g Chocolate Buttercream

3½ oz/100 g pale gray fondant

Confectioners'/icing sugar, for dusting

8 chunky soft licorice sticks

Several pale soft fudge candies/sweets

Handful of toasted flaked almonds

¼ cup/40 g milk chocolate chips

Tube of green decorator frosting/icing

8 mini white candies or sprinkles

Several soft orange fruit chews

SPECIAL EQUIPMENT
Small paper or plastic piping bag

Preheat the oven to 375°F/190°C/gas mark 5. Line a baking sheet with parchment paper. Trace and cut out the Hagrid's Hut Gingerbread Cookies **template** on page 91. Thinly roll out the **dough** (see page 84) on a lightly floured surface and cut around the template. Transfer to the baking sheet and shape more cookies in the same way. Re-roll the trimmings and make more cookies. You'll need eight for this recipe.

Bake the **cookies** for 15 minutes until golden and leave to cool on the baking sheet. Once cooled, transfer the cookies to a board. Spread the top of each one with a thin layer of **chocolate buttercream** (see page 88). Try to avoid the frosting going over the edges.

3

Cut the **template** along the dotted line so that you can use the roof section. Thinly roll out the **gray fondant** on a surface dusted with **confectioners' sugar**. Gently rest the template on the fondant and cut around with a small sharp knife. Position the fondant on the roof area of the **cookie**, pressing down gently. Cover the remaining cookies in the same way and put the fondant trimmings to one side.

4

Cut the **licorice** into flat pieces and trim if necessary to 1¼ × ½ inch/3 × 1 cm lengths. Place one on each of the **cookies** for the front door.

5

Slice the **soft fudge candies** into ⅛ inch/3 mm slices. Cut out and position narrow strips for the door's trim and 1 × ½ inch/2.5 × 1 cm rectangles for the steps. Break the **almonds** into tiny pieces with your fingers and arrange on each side of the door for the stonework.

6

Melt the **chocolate chips** (see page 89) and place in a paper or plastic piping bag. Snip off the very tip so the chocolate can be piped in a fine line. Pipe additional features onto the cookies such as the roof sections, windows, and lines on the doorsteps. Pipe a tiny dot of icing onto the doors and secure a **white candy or sprinkle** for the doorknobs.

7

Roll the **gray fondant** trimmings into small pea-sized pieces and press one into the bottom corners of each cookie for the house supports. Knead a **soft fruit candy** between your fingers to shape a small pumpkin. You'll probably need to halve or quarter each candy first, depending on their size. Position by the steps.

8

Use the **decorator frosting** to pipe grass and detail on the pumpkin.

TOP TIP Because these little cookies are a bit fiddly, you might want to make them a day ahead. Once made, place on a small tray and cover with plastic wrap.

77

QUIDDITCH COOKIES

Quidditch hoops, Bludgers, Quaffles, and the elusive Golden Snitch—this recipe has everything you need for a cracking game of Quidditch (except for the pitch itself). These cute cookies are very easy to decorate and are a great starter recipe if you haven't done much baking before. And just like the ever-popular wizarding sport, the more you practice the better you'll get!

1 HOUR, PLUS CHILLING   **12–15 MINS**   **MAKES ABOUT 16–18**

10 oz/300 g Sugar Cookie/ Biscuit Dough

1 tsp egg white, lightly whisked

1¾ cups/220 g confectioners'/icing sugar

3–4 tsp lemon juice or water

1 small piece of rice paper

Multicolored sprinkles

Yellow or gold sugar sprinkles

Black and red natural food coloring

Black sprinkles

1–2 lengths of soft red fruit string or laces

SPECIAL EQUIPMENT

3 inch/7.5 cm, 2¼ inch/ 5.5 cm, and 1½ inch/4 cm round cookie cutters

3 wooden Popsicle/ ice lolly sticks

Line a large baking sheet with parchment paper. Roll out the **dough** (see page 84) on a lightly floured surface. Cut out three circles using the 3 inch/7.5 cm cutter and transfer to the baking sheet. Cut out the centers using the 1½ inch/4 cm cutter to shape rings.

Place the small circles on the baking sheet for the Snitches. Dip the tips of the Popsicle sticks into the **egg white**, then push them gently into the rings, reshaping the dough around the sticks to make the Quidditch hoops.

MAGICAL FACT

The Harry Potter design team tried out several versions of the Golden Snitch before settling on the gold-plated version we see in the films. One of the prototypes even had insect wings!

Cut out three **cookies** from the rest of the **dough** using the large cutter. Use the same cutter to cut out three little sections from the sides of the cookies to shape the Quaffles and place them on the baking sheet. Cut out three more cookies from the remaining dough using the 2¼ inch/5.5 cm cutter for the Bludgers. Chill the cookies for 30 minutes.

Beat the **confectioners' sugar** and 3 teaspoons **lemon juice or water** in a bowl until smooth. Add a little extra water if needed. The icing should have a thin, spreadable consistency.

Preheat the oven to 375°F/190°C/gas mark 5. Bake the **cookies** for about 12–15 minutes or until golden around the edges. Leave to cool on the baking sheet. While the cookies are cooling, use the Quidditch Cookies wing **template** on page 92 to trace and cut out six wings on your **rice paper**. Drizzle a little **icing** over the hoop cookies and sprinkle with plenty of **multicolored sprinkles**.

Spread more **icing** on the smallest **cookies**. Push two **rice paper wings** into the edges of each and sprinkle with **yellow or gold sugar sprinkles**. Divide the remaining icing between two small bowls.

Create dark gray **icing** by mixing a few drops of **black food coloring** into one bowl. Spread the gray icing onto the Bludger **cookies** and sprinkle with a thin, wavy line of **black sprinkles**.

Mix a few drops of **red food coloring** into the second bowl. To make a deeper, darker red, you can add a drop of **black food coloring** too. Spread the Quaffle **cookies** with the red **icing**. Decorate these with short lengths of **red fruit string or laces** as in the photograph, using scissors to cut pieces to fit. Leave to set for a couple hours before serving.

HOGSMEADE WINTER WARMERS

There are few more enchanting sights than a snowy Hogsmeade. Harry and his friends even have a snowball fight when visiting in the third film! Now you can create your own version of the wizarding village with these stunning little gingerbread houses. But think twice before adding a Shrieking Shack—that place is scary!

 2 HOURS 15 MINS MAKES 16

 14 oz/400 g Gingerbread Cookie/Biscuit Dough

Several chocolate soft chewy candies or toffees

Handful of orange and yellow soft chewy candies/sweets

Tubes of pink, green, and white decorator frosting/icing

7 oz/200 g Royal Icing

SPECIAL EQUIPMENT

Paper or plastic piping bag

1

Line a baking sheet with parchment paper. Trace and cut out the three Hogsmeade Winter Warmers **templates** on page 91. On a lightly floured surface, thinly roll out the **dough** (see page 84) and cut around the templates, one at a time. Transfer to the baking sheet. Repeat with the remaining dough. Re-roll the trimmings and cut out more shapes in the same way. There should be enough dough to make 16 cookies. Chill the dough while you preheat the oven to 375°F/190°C/gas mark 5.

Bake the **cookies** for 15 minutes until slightly darker around the edges. Leave to cool on the baking sheet. Cut thin slices of the **chocolate chewy candies** and position on the cookies for doors. You might need to cut them down to the right size, depending on the candies you use. Shape and position the other house features like the triangular decorations over the upper windows and longer rectangles over the lower windows.

Flatten the soft **orange and yellow candies** with your fingers or a rolling pin and cut into little squares and rectangles with scissors or a small knife for the windows. Press into position.

Use the tubes of **pink, green, and white decorator frosting** to pipe panes of glass and frames onto the windows. Use more of the frosting to pipe doorknobs, door wreaths, and brickwork.

Put the **royal icing** (see page 89) in a piping bag and snip a little off the tip so the icing can be piped in a thick line. Use this to pipe snow onto the rooftops as shown in the photograph. Pipe a little more at the tops of the chimneys and along the bases of the cookies.

MAGICAL FACT

The Harry Potter film set designers decided to locate Hogsmeade high in a mountain, above the tree line, keeping the village's iconic rooftops covered in snow all year long!

BASIC RECIPES

Sugar Cookies
Gingerbread Cookies
Chocolate Brownies
Sponge Cake and Cupcakes
Buttercream Frosting
Royal Icing
Melting Chocolate

SUGAR COOKIES

A delicious and useful recipe that can be decorated with all types of frostings, from chocolate and buttercream to fondant and royal Icing.

15 MINS PLUS CHILLING	15 MINS	MAKES 10 OZ/300 G

1¼ cups/155 g all-purpose/plain flour

Pinch of salt

⅞ stick/90 g firm unsalted butter, diced

⅓ cup/40 g confectioners'/icing sugar

I large egg yolk

I tsp vanilla extract

Put the flour, salt, and butter in a bowl and use your fingertips to rub the butter into the flour until the mixture looks like breadcrumbs. (Alternatively, blend the ingredients together in a food processor.) Add the sugar, egg yolk, and vanilla and mix to a smooth, firm dough. Wrap in plastic wrap and chill for about 30 minutes until firm. Roll out your dough and cut out cookie shapes following your chosen recipe.

⟩ CHOCOLATE VARIATION ⟨

For Chocolate Cookies: replace ¼ cup/30 g of flour with ¼ cup/30 g unsweetened cocoa powder.

TOP TIP

Cookie dough contains plenty of butter, which softens in a warm kitchen. If the dough becomes soft and sticky as you try to shape it, simply put it back in the fridge for about 20 minutes, then try again. Don't waste the leftover trimmings. Roll them up into a ball, chill to firm, and roll again to make more delicious cookies.

TOP TIP

While the cookie mix is chilling, use the time to gather the ingredients you need for your chosen recipe and cut out a template if you're using one. You can also line a baking sheet with parchment paper so you're ready to go!

GINGERBREAD COOKIES

Gingerbread cookies are usually made at Christmastime, but if you like the flavor, why not make them any time of year? These cookies are delicious with all types of frostings.

15 MINS PLUS CHILLING	15 MINS	MAKES 14 OZ/400 G

1½ cups/190 g all-purpose/plain flour

¼ tsp baking powder

Good pinch of salt

I tsp ground ginger

½ tsp ground cinnamon

¾ stick/85 g firm unsalted butter, diced

I large egg yolk

⅓ cup/75 g light brown/muscovado sugar

3 tbsp black treacle or molasses/syrup

Put the flour, baking powder, salt, ginger, cinnamon, and butter in a bowl and use your fingertips to rub the butter into the flour until the mixture looks like breadcrumbs. (Alternatively, blend the ingredients together in a food processor.) Add the egg yolk, sugar, and black treacle or molasses and mix to a smooth, firm dough. Wrap in plastic wrap and chill for about 30 minutes until firm. Roll out your dough and cut out cookie shapes following your chosen recipe.

CHOCOLATE BROWNIES

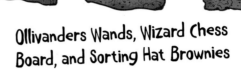

This clever mixture can be baked as a slab in the traditional way before cutting into pieces, or made into little cupcakes instead. Simply make the mixture below and then follow the individual recipes for the required pan size and baking time.

🕐 20 MINS   🍴🍽 SERVES 12

1½ cups/225 g dark chocolate chips

1½ sticks/170 g unsalted butter, diced

3 large eggs, beaten

1 cup/220 g light brown/muscovado sugar

¾ cup/95 g all-purpose/plain flour

½ tsp baking powder

1 cup/150 g milk chocolate chips

Preheat the oven to 375°F/190°C/gas mark 5. Put the chocolate chips and butter in a heatproof bowl and rest the bowl over a saucepan of gently simmering water. When the chocolate has melted, stir to make a smooth mixture. In a separate bowl, whisk together the eggs and sugar with a handheld electric mixer for about 3–4 minutes until it is much paler in color and foamy. Stir in the chocolate mixture. Sift the flour and baking powder into the bowl, add the milk chocolate, and stir gently until mixed.

Ollivanders Wands, Wizard Chess Board, and Sorting Hat Brownies

Grease and line a 9 inch/23 cm square cake pan/tin with parchment paper. Scrape the brownie mixture into the tin and spread level. Bake for 40 minutes until a sugary crust has formed on the surface. A toothpick inserted into the center should come out with a few moist crumbs. Leave to cool in the tin.

Acromantula Cupcake Stack

Line a 12-section muffin tray with paper liners. Divide the mixture among the liners until two-thirds full. Bake for 25 minutes until lightly set. Leave to cool in the tray.

SPONGE CAKE AND CUPCAKES

This super-easy all-in-one sponge cake mix can be adapted to make all the cakes and cupcakes in this book. Simply make the mixture below and then follow the individual recipe list for the pan size and baking times you'll need.

 10 MINS   **SERVES 10-12**

1¾ sticks/195 g unsalted butter, softened

⅞ cup/175 g caster sugar

3 large eggs, beaten

2 tsp vanilla extract

1½ cups/190 g all-purpose/plain flour

2 tsp baking powder

Preheat the oven to 350°F/180°C/gas mark 4. Beat together the butter, sugar, eggs, vanilla extract, flour, and baking powder with a handheld electric mixer until smooth and creamy. This will take about 2 minutes.

⋛ CHOCOLATE VARIATION ⋚

For a chocolate cake, replace ¼ cup/30 g of flour with ¼ cup/30 g cocoa powder. (Don't do this for the Knight Bus Layer Cake, though, or the purple layers won't show!)

Bertie Bott's Every Flavour Beans Box and Deathly Hallows Cake

Grease an **11 x 7 inch/28 x 18 cm cake pan** or shallow baking tin with a little melted butter and line with a rectangle of parchment paper. Transfer the cake mixture to the tin and spread level, making sure it goes right into the corners. (For the Deathly Hallows Cake, use the chocolate variation for the batter.) Bake for **35 minutes** until the surface feels just firm to the touch. Leave to cool in the pan for **10 minutes**.

Hogwarts: A History, Hogwarts House Scarf, and Marauder's Map Cakes

Grease a **10 x 8 inch/25.5 x 20 cm cake pan** or shallow baking tin with a little melted butter and line with a rectangle of parchment paper. For the Marauder's Map Cake, use an **11 x 7 inch/28 x 18 cm cake pan** instead. Transfer the cake mixture to the tin and spread level making sure it goes right into the corners. Bake for **35 minutes** until the surface feels just firm to the touch. Leave to cool in the pan for **10 minutes**.

TOP TIP

If you don't have got time to make the cake and decorate it all in one session, make the cake the day before. Once it has cooled, wrap in kitchen foil or plastic wrap overnight. You could even make it further ahead, wrap, and freeze it.

Cauldron Cake

Grease three **6 inch/15 cm round/sandwich pans** and line the bases with circles of parchment paper. Divide the cake mixture among the tins and spread level. Bake **20-25 minutes** until the surface feels just firm to the touch. Leave to cool in the pans for **10 minutes.**

Harry's Birthday Cake

Grease two **8 inch/20 cm round/sandwich pans** and line the bases with circles of parchment paper. Divide the cake mixture between the tins and spread level. Bake for **25 minutes** until the surface feels just firm to the touch. Leave to cool in the pans for **10 minutes.**

Knight Bus Layer Cake

Grease a **10 x 8 inch/25.5 x 20 cm cake pan** or shallow baking tin with a little melted butter and line with a rectangle of parchment paper. Transfer the cake mixture to the tin and spread level. Bake for **35 minutes** until the surface feels just firm to the touch. Leave to cool in the pan for **10 minutes.**
Make another cake in the same way, adding a few drops of purple food coloring to the batter before baking.

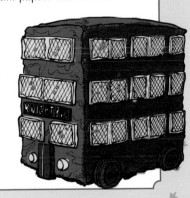

CUPCAKES

Forbidden Forest Fancies, Gringotts Dragon, Platform 9¾ Cupcakes, Pygmy Puffs, Pumpkin Patch Cake, and *Mimbulus Mimbletonia*

Line a **12-section cupcake/muffin pan** with paper liners. (Check with your chosen recipe to see what color paper liners you need.) Spoon in the batter until each liner is two-thirds full. Bake for about **20-25 minutes** until the cupcakes have risen and are just firm to the touch. Leave to cool in the tray.

Welcome Feast Illusion Cake

Grease and line two **7 x 3½ inch/18 x 9 cm loaf pans** or baking tins (or similar size). Divide the cake mixture between the tins and spread level. Bake for **25-30 minutes** until the surface feels just firm to the touch. Leave to cool in the pans for **10 minutes.**

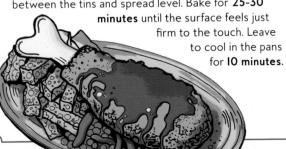

FROSTINGS

Here are the delicious toppings, fillings, and frostings you'll need to decorate your cakes, cupcakes, cookies, and brownies. This is where the fun really starts!

BUTTERCREAM FROSTING

This is a versatile and delicious frosting that you can use as a filling, to cover an entire cake, or for piping decorations. Choose the quantity you need below.

Makes 7 oz/200 g:

²/₃ stick/75 g unsalted butter, softened

I cup/125 g confectioners'/icing sugar

½ tsp vanilla extract

Chocolate Buttercream:

I tsp hot water

⅛ cup/15 g cocoa powder

Makes 12 oz/350 g:

I¼ sticks/135 g unsalted butter, softened

I¾ cups/220 g confectioners'/icing sugar

I tsp vanilla extract

Chocolate Buttercream:

2 tsp hot water

¼ cup/30 g cocoa powder

Put the butter, sugar, and vanilla extract in a bowl and whisk until the mixture is paler in color. Scrape the mixture down from the sides of the bowl halfway through so it's evenly mixed. Add the hot water and cocoa powder, if making Chocolate Buttercream, and mix again for several minutes until very creamy.

ROYAL ICING

Made using just confectioners' sugar and egg whites, royal icing is perfect for more skilled decorations and can be used for spreading and piping. It can also be thinned and "flooded" over cookies for a very professional-looking result!

I large egg white

Approximately 1½ cups/190 g confectioners'/icing sugar, sifted

Put the egg white in a bowl and lightly whisk to break it up. Beat in the sugar, a little at a time, until the icing is thickened and very smooth. It's ready when it holds its shape in little peaks when the whisk is lifted from the bowl. Cover the surface with plastic wrap until ready to use to prevent a crust forming.

TOP TIP

The consistency of royal icing will vary depending on the exact volume of the egg white used. For piping in a thin line, the consistency should be softly peaking. For flooding into cookies, it should be a consistency that slowly becomes level in the bowl when left to stand for a few seconds. If you need to thin the icing, add a little water, drop by drop, until you have the desired consistency.

TOP TIP

You can use egg white powder instead of fresh egg whites in royal icing. Simply add 5 g egg white powder with the 1½ cups/190 g confectioners'/icing sugar and whisk with 2-2½ tablespoons cold water until smooth.

MELTING CHOCOLATE

To melt chocolate, place chocolate chips in a heatproof bowl and rest the bowl over a small pan of very gently simmering water until the chocolate starts to melt. Continue to heat the chocolate, stirring frequently until completely smooth with no lumps remaining. Alternatively, microwave on medium power, in short spurts, stirring frequently until smooth.

TEMPLATES

Trace these templates and cut them out to use on your bakes!

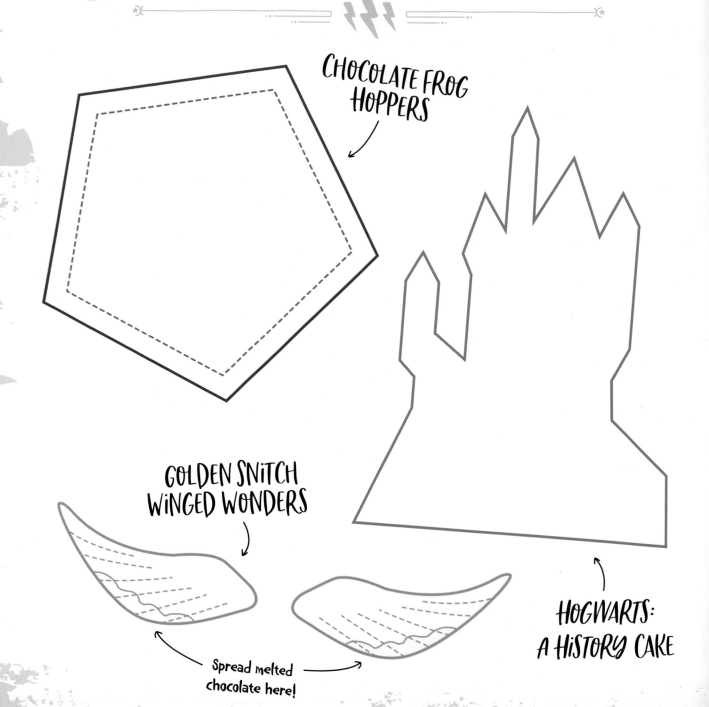

CHOCOLATE FROG HOPPERS

GOLDEN SNITCH WINGED WONDERS

HOGWARTS: A HISTORY CAKE

Spread melted chocolate here!

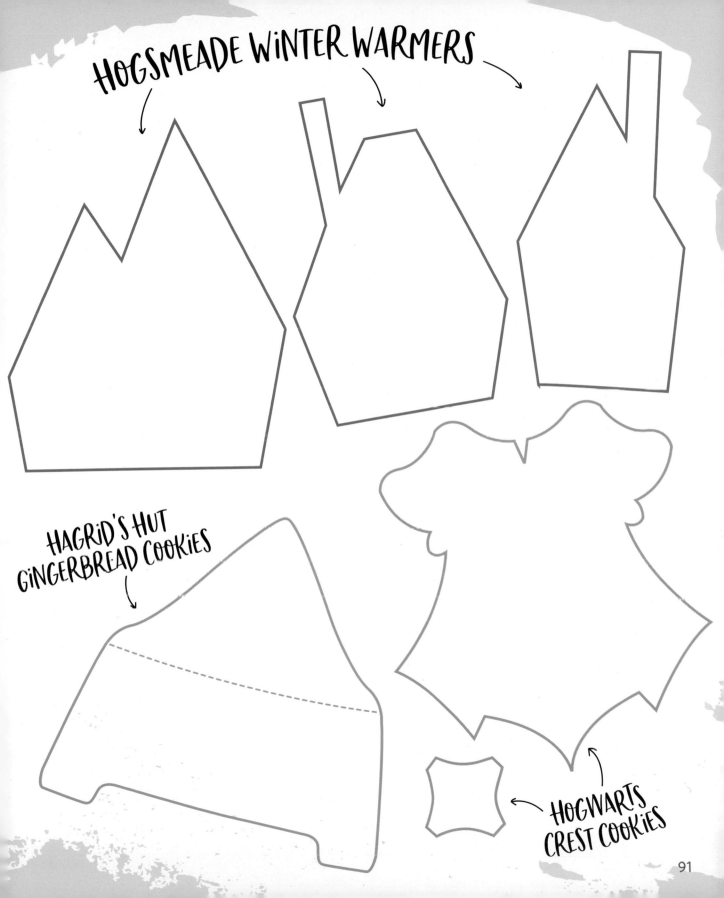

HOGSMEADE WINTER WARMERS

HAGRID'S HUT
GINGERBREAD COOKIES

HOGWARTS
CREST COOKIES

HOGWARTS STAINED-GLASS WINDOWS

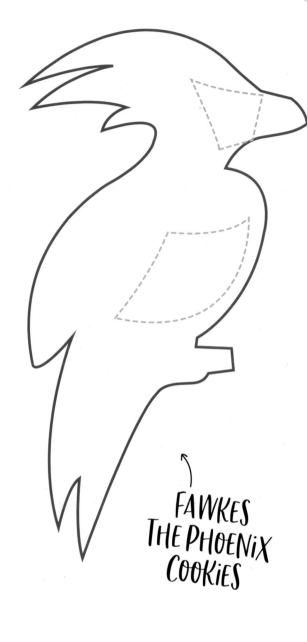

FAWKES
THE PHOENIX
COOKIES

QUIDDITCH COOKIES

MEASUREMENT CONVERSION CHARTS

WEIGHT

IMPERIAL	METRIC
½ oz	15 g
1 oz	29 g
2 oz	57 g
3 oz	85 g
4 oz	113 g
5 oz	141 g
6 oz	170 g
8 oz	227 g
10 oz	283 g
12 oz	340 g
14 oz	397 g
1 lb	453 g

LIQUID WEIGHT

CUPS	OZ	ML
1 tbsp	½ fl oz	15 ml
⅛ cup	1 fl oz	30 ml
¼ cup	2 fl oz	60 ml
⅓ cup	2½ fl oz	80 ml
½ cup	4 fl oz	120 ml
¾ cup	6 fl oz	175 ml
1 cup	8 fl oz	240 ml
1½ cups	12 fl oz	355 ml
1¾ cups	14 fl oz	415 ml
2 cups	16 fl oz	480 ml
2½ cups	20 fl oz	590 ml
3 cups	24 fl oz	710 ml

TEMPERATURE

FAHRENHEIT	CELSIUS
100°F	37°C
150°F	65°C
200°F	93°C
250°F	121°C
300°F	150°C
325°F	160°C
350°F	180°C
375°F	190°C
400°F	200°C
425°F	220°C
450°F	230°C
500°F	260°C

NOTE: All conversions are approximate

LIQUID CONVERSIONS

1 GALLON
4 quarts
8 pints
16 cups
128 fl oz
3.8 liters

1 QUART
2 pints
4 cups
32 fl oz
946 ml

1 PINT
2 cups
16 fl oz
473 ml

1 CUP
16 tbsp
8 fl oz
237 ml

¼ CUP
4 tbsp
2 fl oz
60 ml

1 tsp = 5 ml

1 tbsp = 15 ml

TOP TIP

When measuring using a cup, remember that dry ingredients should be leveled rather than piled up in the center of the cup.

If you measure wet ingredients first, rinse and dry the cup before measuring dry ingredients, otherwise the dry ingredients might stick to the cup.

INDEX

Scholastic Inc., 557 Broadway, New York, NY 10012

Scholastic UK Ltd., 1 London Bridge, London, SE1 9BG

Scholastic Ireland, 89E Lagan Road, Dublin Industrial Estate, Glasnevin, Dublin, D11 HP5F

ISBN 978-1-339-05302-8

10 9 8 7 6 5 4 3 2 1   24 25 26 27 28

Printed in China   84

First printing 2024

Supplementary imagery © Shutterstock

AMAZING15, Project Management and Design
JOANNA FARROW, Writer and Food Styling
KATE LLOYD, Additional Writing and Copy Editing
KIRSTEN MURRAY, Additional Writing
LIZ & MAX HAARALA HAMILTON, Photography
REBECCA WOODS, Food Styling
BETHANY STRAKER, Illustrations (pages 84-89)

Thank you to our models:
Adam, Alexis, Coco, Dayne, Farrah, Francesca, Imogen, Izaiah, Kasia, Megan, Tate, and Travis

Special thanks to:
Alysia Scudamore and Sam Sorbello at Urban Angels, and Vanessa Bird

SAMANTHA SWANK, Editor, Scholastic · **SALENA MAHINA**, Art Direction, Scholastic
VICTORIA SELOVER, Director – Editorial Publishing, Warner Bros. Discovery
KATIE CAMPBELL, Senior Design Manager – Global Publishing, Warner Bros. Discovery
LUKE BARNARD, Product Development Manager – The Blair Partnership
HOLLY CAVILL, Brand and Franchise Executive - The Blair Partnership